THINGS THAT MAKE FOR PEACE

*Would that even today
you knew the things
that make for peace.*

LUKE 19:42

THINGS THAT MAKE FOR PEACE

*A personal search for
a new way of life*

JOHN & MARY SCHRAMM

AUGSBURG PUBLISHING HOUSE
MINNEAPOLIS, MINNESOTA

To our many friends,
especially in the Order of St. Martin,
who help us understand gospel values

THINGS THAT MAKE FOR PEACE

154950

CONTENTS

Preface

This book flows from our life. It is not the story of our lives, but is nevertheless a personal account. For a decade we have been learning that peace is a lifestyle. This truth became clear in the process of recording these reflections.

Many today are interested in peace—whether that be the elimination of armed conflict in the global setting, a sense of tranquility within their lives, or an elimination of injustice in a world of extreme disparities. Therefore there are peace studies at an increasing number of universities, books on peace of mind, techniques for obtaining tranquility, and leaders in church and state calling us to change our way of life because we are living in a hungry world.

Most of the assumptions behind "peace talk" seem to make peace the goal to be sought—whether that is inner tranquility or cessation of fighting. We think it is important to begin with a different assumption: *peace is a lifestyle*. A. J. Muste said it well: "There is no way to peace, peace is the way." This book is the journal of two people who have been taking a long time in finding this to be true.

We have chosen the format of a journal for several reasons. It feels less presumptuous for us to write about peace in this form. It is presumptuous to think our journals were noteworthy enough to be published, but a journal is honestly noting what one has heard, read, observed, and felt. Therefore since so much of our experience of peace and the peace issues has come through other people's lives, comments, and writings, all we do here is share those with you.

Some of the incidents have specific historic reference and were recorded in our journals. Others came to mind as we wrote and had been recorded only in our memories. In order to provide some coherence for the reader, we have grouped entries by topic more than by chronology.

As is the case in any journal, more entries come from what others have said or written than from profound personal insights. We extend our apologies to anyone from whom we have taken ideas without remembering the source or giving proper credit.

We hope that the sharing of our thoughts will lead you to examine your own life and to think more deeply about the things that make for peace.

When Peace Was a Fighting Word

May Day, 1970: Today we found ourselves literally and figuratively in the middle of the peace movement. By mid-morning came the radio announcement that the conflict between the D.C. Police and students, protesting the American invasion of Cambodia, had peaked and was receding. "One of the few confrontations remaining is in the 1300 block of 21st Street," the announcer said. Our row house is in the middle of that block.

We insisted the kids go to school. The streets and sidewalks were crowded with college students heading toward the White House with placards and banners, but it seemed safe enough. It wasn't until Mark came running back, saying he wanted to stay home, that John and I realized the seriousness of the situation. The police were coming down 21st Street in waves, brandishing clubs, shouting through bullhorns, trying to disperse the crowd. Commuters from suburban Maryland found themselves barely able to creep down the one-way street.

"You are inconveniencing me!" a man shouted from his Lincoln Continental.

"War is also an inconvenience," a student retorted.

With a few choice expletives the driver demanded the students get out of his way. During the verbal battle that followed, the irate man jumped out of his car to chase the bearded youth challenging him. As he left his car someone turned off the ignition and locked the door with the key inside. The police quickly bore down on the group, and one student was singled out to be brought to his knees with blows from a club.

The battered and bloody head changed the scene in front of our steps. What had begun as a peaceful march —protesting killing and violence—degenerated rapidly. Trash cans were overturned and set afire. V.W.s and any other compact cars parked along the curbs, were set sideways in the street. Sirens and more bullhorn orders, chasing, clubbing, angry shouts, and warnings followed.

I felt nauseated and my emotions fluctuated from excitement, to horror and to frustration. We had a strange, uneasy feeling we were watching a football game somehow out of control. We found ourselves taking sides and secretly applauding any points scored by the students.

Other neighbors viewing the scene from their front steps felt differently. The middle-aged woman, who marched across the street after the students had been arrested and herded into police vans, shook her fist in our faces and her voice quivered with emotion. "What kind of parents are you," she hissed, "allowing your children to watch this. Look what those hoodlums did to the ivy next to my steps!"

We wonder what kind of parents we are. Our kids know how we feel about the effects of war, and any comparison of its ravages to damage done to the lady's ivy, or to the inconvenience of our suburban commuters, seems ludicrous.

Driving across the Potomac River on Memorial Bridge we came abreast of a dilapidated car with the bumper sticker, "War is not healthy for children and other living things." We honked our horn, smiled, and gave the peace sign of two fingers upward in a V. The occupants of the car responded with wide grins and returned the peace sign.

In the next lane over, the lone occupant of a third car, after seeing our peace greetings, sped quickly in front of the dilapidated car. Exhibiting a clenched fist, he swerved his car sharply to cut directly in front of them. The bumper sticker on his car read "America, love it or leave it."

The incident and the two bumper stickers are vivid reminders that peace can be a fighting word.

Though we are living in the middle of the peace movement, it is more geographical than ideological. By background we are good Lutherans. Our just-war position has meant that we supported our government's involvement in World War II and Korea. At least there had been no great questioning done in our homes, church, or schools. Romans 13 had settled the conscience question: we were "subject to the powers that be for they are ordained of God." I can even remember my catechism instruction that said the difficult choices are not between

11

good and evil, but between good and better, or bad and worse. In war one chooses the lesser of two evils.

But the Vietnam struggle has brought out other questions—other Scripture texts.

The floor debate at the church convention in Minneapolis centered on selective conscientious objection. The young people speaking for it out of personal conviction and immediate concern were criticized because of the "selective" quality. In essence they were accused of being against the Vietnam war because this is the one in which they have to fight. They were accused of being selective out of self-interest and cowardice.

These criticisms seem to miss the heart of the Lutheran tradition and heritage. If there is one appropriate stance for Lutherans at a time of war, it would be "selectivity." This is the response of a just-war ethic. The just-war, or justifiable-war, criteria imply that some wars are just and some are not. Therefore the Christian is called to repeated decision-making rather than to any absolutist position.

The speakers for conscientious objection to the war in Vietnam have some convincing arguments. Since Cicero refined the first formulations of Plato, all criteria for justifiable wars have included that it must be *declared by a legitimate authority,* and this conflict hasn't been declared at all. It is also difficult to say that *all peaceful means of solution have been exhausted,* that the war is now undertaken as a last resort.

Perhaps the sharpest criticism of the Vietnam war comes under the *principle of proportionality:* the good resulting from fighting should outweigh the evil done by the fighting. When the military announced concerning the city of Ben Tre, "We had to destroy the city in order to save it," all proportionality seemed to have been lost. It also seems that the criteria of *all moderation, no harm to non-combatants, no widespread devastation,* have become obsolete in our modern warfare. There is a general erosion of moral constraint which has been at the heart of the just-war ethic.

My reaction to the debate this afternoon was to question more seriously our involvement in Vietnam and to understand more thoughtfully the young people who speak as conscientious objectors. I am also aware of just how little I knew about our own Lutheran position. I didn't even know the just-war criteria.

This evening I went with Rod to a meeting in Crafton of young people interested in community action. He led a discussion on the church's view of peace and war. The group was anti-church but cordial to us as individual church members. On many points of criticism I found it difficult to defend the church.

I thought one comment most profound. A young man said, "The church has been for peace between wars. That's like being a vegetarian between meals."

It's ironic that the church can be so concerned about the morality of sex, alcohol, tobacco, and remain so silent about the morality of issues that are literally life and death—war, justice, racism, oppression.

During recent months I have come to see more and more the need for the method of nonviolence in international relations. While I was convinced during my student days of the power of nonviolence in group conflicts within nations, I was not yet convinced of its efficacy in conflicts

13

between nations. I felt that while war could never be a positive or absolute good, it could serve as a negative good in the sense of preventing the spread and growth of an evil force. War, I felt, horrible as it is, might be preferable to surrender to a totalitarian system. But more and more I have come to the conclusion that the potential destructiveness of modern weapons of war totally rules out the possibility of war ever serving again as a negative good. If we assume that mankind has a right to survive then we must find an alternative to war and destruction. . . . The choice is no longer between violence and nonviolence. It is either nonviolence or nonexistence.

I am no doctrinaire pacifist. I have tried to embrace a realistic pacifism. Moreover, I see the pacifist position not as sinless but as the lesser evil in the circumstances. Therefore I do not claim to be free from the moral dilemmas that the Christian nonpacifist confronts. But I am convinced that the church cannot remain silent while mankind faces the threat of being plunged into the abyss of nuclear annihilation.

MARTIN LUTHER KING, Jr.

When nominations are sought for peace-wagers, I have a candidate. Dick is a Jesuit priest who lives, talks, eats and works for peace. It is an inspiration to see such a "purity of heart, to will one thing."

It was illustrated in a phone call today. Laura told me she called Dick on the phone and could hardly hear his voice. She inquired about this and discovered that he was ill with flu, sore throat, and laryngitis. She asked him if there was anything she could do.

The answer came back—just a whisper but unmistakably clear—"Yes, work for peace in Vietnam."

14

We had invited four couples to dinner. The same evening there was to be another demonstration against the Vietnam war. The march was to begin at DuPont Circle, two blocks from our home. *The Washington Post* reported the demonstrators had difficulty securing a march permit because the Vietnamese Embassy was to be the demonstration target.

Dinner parties are enjoyable occasions. Between cocktails and dessert one can be in the company of friends, forgetting for a time the world outside, or, if desired, solving all the world's problems. Tonight we had chosen to be mentally uninvolved in heavy issues. The conversation was light, stereo music and candlelight tranquilizing our moods.

At nine o'clock this mood was shattered. The sound of sirens, running feet, and bullhorns brought us hurrying to the front door. The air outside was pungent, stifling. We gagged, and as our eyes began to burn, we realized tear gas had been used to break up the demonstration. A few of the demonstrators—maybe infiltrators, maybe not—had thrown rocks through the window of a nearby bank. The police had responded rapidly to bring the situation under control. Those few who had initiated the violence had come prepared with gas masks and wet cloths, but the rest of the demonstrators were totally unprepared and found themselves hurrying for cover.

We stuffed a towel in the front window and laid a rug in front of the door.

Dave said what we were all thinking. "Let's face it. The world seeps in around you, like or not."

Dottie has another sticker on her front door. This one says "Trail of broken treaties." Her door advertises her concerns: A Gene McCarthy daisy. A blue and white dove with the words "Work for Peace." Boycott lettuce. Welfare Rights. Boycott grapes. D.C., Last Colony.

Like many of our friends we move from one battle-field to another. We protest, pray, write letters, lobby and campaign for candidates we feel understand peace and justice. On several occasions our basement has been wall-to-wall sleeping bags. Harvard, Yale, Columbia students, whose names we can't even remember, have slept in our home when they have come to join a nonviolent protest against the war.

The world around us shouts of wrongs to be righted, of injustices, of wounds to be healed, of causes to be promoted. Any person with a conscience cannot live in the milieu of the '60s and fail to be drawn into some area of Christian concern. But where does one begin? How do we pick and choose? More important, where do we draw the line?

We are still uncomfortable that issues of peace and justice can cause so much hostility and anger. Some problems to which we felt we needed to respond have caused friction with some of our neighbors. Our small, developing congregation is committed to civil rights and working for a just peace in Vietnam. It is obvious to us that neighbors who are established Washingtonians regret that they welcomed with open arms the new preacher and his family who moved into their block. At one time two petitions were circulating around the neighborhood—one to get rid of the rats and the other to get rid of our congregation.

A neighbor who saw someone break into our basement and steal Mike's bike did nothing about it because, as he later yelled across the fence, "It's what you deserve!"

16

An elderly lady called to warn us that our children would get all kinds of diseases playing with black children. "And," she raged, "if you think you are beautifying Washington with niggers in your yard, you've got another think coming!"

Jesus was clear enough when he warned his disciples they would have to face tribulations in this world. I am certainly not ready for any big test of my faithfulness because even small criticisms disturb me. Confrontations with neighbors and friends and associates leave me shaking inside. I have not learned to deal with these hostile situations and find my firm convictions eroding under a battery of loud vocal shots and snide remarks.

If a man happens to be 36 years old, as I happen to be, and some great truth stands before the door of his life, some great opportunity to stand up for that which is right and that which is just, and he refuses to stand up because he wants to live a little longer and he is afraid his home will get bombed, or he is afraid that he will get shot . . . he may go on and live until he's 80, and the cessation of breathing in his life is merely the belated announcement of an earlier death of the spirit.

Man dies when he refuses to stand up for that which is right. A man dies when he refuses to take a stand for that which is true. So we are going to stand up right here . . . letting the world know we are determined to be free.
MARTIN LUTHER KING, JR.

The ideas some people have of the "peace movement" and the stereotypes of "peace" people continue to surprise me. Suburban friends, relatives from the Midwest, and other pastors seem to share such misconceptions. Almost every experience I have had in the demonstrations has been of peaceful protest. The crowd is more like a Sunday school gathering than an angry mob. The violence is limited to an extremely small fraction of people. I laid my coat on the ground this afternoon when the sun got hot and realized that others in the demonstration—and there were several hundred thousand—even had the thoughtfulness to respect such a small thing as a jacket on the ground.

Perhaps one cause of this misrepresentation is that the news media report only the dramatic. Often it is the isolated violent incident that gets news coverage. But I don't get too critical of the reporters. I find that for the most part I remember the exceptional and the dramatic. Even my own journal contains more of the dramatic than the ordinary. But it's too bad. This helps to maintain the strong devisiveness in our country regarding the issues themselves.

When the issues of peace are so explosive, the role of pastor becomes difficult but extremely important. I wish more of us could share the fine balance Roy has. Last Sunday morning in his sermon he commented on the Cambodian invasion and explained why he had permitted Lutheran students, coming to Washington to protest, to sleep in the church basement.

Reactions to the students, the protest, and the sermon were mixed and strong. One man would hardly extend his hand to the pastor in the traditional front door ritual. He said with great emotion, "I'm so angry I can hardly talk."

Roy responded, "Could you by Wednesday night?"

The man didn't quite understand, so Roy repeated, "Do

you think you'd cool down enough by Wednesday that we could talk it through?''

They did just that.

I think both actions are commendable: the courage to take a stand and make the protest, and also to spend the time with those who disagree or don't understand.

Both are pastoral acts.

Sound the Trumpet in Tekoa

Living in this period of transition from the 1960s into the '70s is like living on Tuesday of Holy Week. In some ways it's the hardest of times. We tend to glorify the past and to want to go back. Do you remember Palm Sunday? A great day with all the crowds on the streets and the excitement of the moment. But on Tuesday, those things are in the past and we know in our honest moments that we can never go back.

On Tuesday there are always some who sense that even greater things are ahead. There are those who have a hint of Easter. The message comes, "If you think last Sunday was something, wait till next week!"

But someone is sure to point out that Friday comes first. You can't get from Palm Sunday to Easter without Friday, and that always means a day of suffering and crucifixion. This day is coming for the church. St. Peter speaks to this when he says, "Do not be surprised at the fiery ordeal which has come upon you." I think this text will take on new meaning in the next few years when the church in America becomes a suffering church as it is today in other parts of the world.

Friday has its challenges and its suffering, but in some ways this Tuesday in which we are living is even more difficult. On Friday the adrenalin flows. We are called to "mount up with wings as eagles." But Tuesday is a time between the times and these are difficult. It is sometimes hardest to "walk and not faint."

In some lectionaries there are no lessons for Tuesday of Holy Week. You either use Monday's lessons again or read the one for Wednesday. How does one live on a day when there is no Word for that day? The only name I can find for Tuesday comes from the parable of the fig tree— Fig Tuesday—it even sounds dreary.

Where are the signals for our day? In what directions are we now called?

A Catholic priest friend who was on the streets in the middle of the activist era remarked, "All my liberal friends are now basket cases."

Events are happening that should demand my attention but I feel mentally, physically, and spiritually stymied. Perhaps I should say some things are *not* happening that have been so much a part of our lives the past five years.

No more students are sleeping on our floors these days. There hasn't been an "envelope stuffing" party in over a year, and political battles have failed to call forth any great commitment on my part. Protest demonstrations are almost non-existent.

No more Saturday night basement meals to prepare for the runaways and counter-culture kids—they've migrated elsewhere. Black leadership has stepped into the civic organization, which is a goal accomplished, but I now find myself less and less involved. The biggest change is that neighbors are no longer circulating petitions against us, in fact they seem apathetic to our existence on the block.

Some of this is a relief, but mostly it is disturbing. I try to analyze what is happening. Am I just tired of "well doing?" Maybe I'm deluding myself that the problems have solved themselves and justice has finally come. Some days I'm sure I just lack the discipline and stamina to see a problem through. I know that Jesus took his stand with the poor and the oppressed. Perhaps I really no longer believe this is the example I want to follow.

I have no answers, just a lot of questions.

Our inner-city congregation, the Community of Christ was born in the middle of the 1960s. We were born in, and became part of, the "activist" era of the church. The issues included race, poverty, war. Those issues are still before us. They have not been solved, and they won't go away. But the mood has changed. The great "liberal" dream about solving them through political actions has become shaky. Robert Lecky speaks to the present situation with these words:

In the present crisis in the church some interesting things are happening. No longer is there the *way to do things. Some of these ministries—remember when campus ministry and inner-city churches was where the action was? —that were going to show us the way of truth and rele-*

vance are now freely conceding that they have no monopoly on these things, in fact they are even a little nervous.

There are several directions which "activists" including the Community of Christ, may take:

The activists may just quit. The need for "liberals" is past, and these people will just become confused and discouraged, even though the issues are still there.

The activists may find new avenues for their energies, apart from the church. This may be acceptable because the issues will still be faced, but not only will the church lose something, the people working separately from a community of faith will lose an important dimension to their involvement.

The activists may slip back into "personal piety." There will be a great attraction in any offer of inner peace. The offers will come from the "Jesus movement" and the pentecostals, from the human potential movement and from the sects which offer techniques in meditation as the new answer to the world's needs. Each of these answers has some truth and validity. When they are a way of avoiding distressing issues, however, they are not a faithful response.

The alternative is to find the new visions for our involvement in the '70s. We must become radical—that is, get at the roots again—and find the spiritual resources for the task.

There have been other times in history when God's people sensed that they needed signals to help discover new directions. It feels like one of those times. Many people are giving advice, but it still seems as if there is no clear signal. The people of Jerusalem sometimes waited for the trumpet to sound from Tekoa as their signal.

Maybe one could see better from this high wilderness spot south of Jerusalem. Whether I understand it fully or not, it makes sense for me to echo Jeremiah: "Sound the trumpet in Tekoa."

The person who remained aloof from the critical issues of the '60s and kept saying the church shouldn't be involved in politics can be of no help to me in these questioning times. His was an easy rationalization for not engaging in the struggles for liberation, human rights, and peace.

Now that we are reassessing everything, this same person comes and says to me "I told you so. I knew the fad of civil rights and peace would pass and you'd realize again the real mission of the church."

Not only can this person not help me, I find myself angry with him. I believe the '60s were years of genuine mission for the church, when we gained a clearer understanding of the gospel. To find new directions we must start from our present position of having come through the years of struggle.

Those who proudly and piously stood back from the struggle can hardly have the answers for today. They don't even have the questions!

The form in which the faith question comes to me is in the area of nonviolence. Usually any signal or direction comes only in real struggling with a question. In the '60s there was a wide acceptance of nonviolence as an underlying strategy for the movement for social change. As I look back on those years, I think I accepted the nonviolence as a tactic more than as a lifestyle. We thought nonviolence could achieve the desired goals. I fear that many of those in the movement would have switched to other methods if it could have been proved that non-violence wouldn't "work." It seems that many of the people working for social justice have now concluded that nonviolence is somewhat naive and unrealistic. The question for me is this: is nonviolence more than a tactic? Does the life and teachings of Jesus call me to a life of nonviolence even if it doesn't work? After all, it really didn't "work" for Jesus: he ended up on a cross. Non-violence is more than a tactic, and in the exploration of it there is the possibility of finding those signals and directions for which I have been looking.

I have been doing a lot of reading on the subject of violence. How one responds to violence continues to be the question that rattles my cage. Sometimes in the past I have run away from the hard questions and busied my-self with something else. It is becoming clearer to me that I can't do that this time. Somehow I know I have to wrestle with this question.

A significant book is Jacques Ellul's *Violence*. Ellul has an interesting style of presentation. The first section of the book is a careful and convincing presentation on the necessity of violence. It is the only reaction possible in a violent world. It is useless to judge whether the violence was right or wrong, it was the only thing one could do.

The twist comes when Ellul presents the nature of Christian freedom as the ability to deny the necessary. Granted that the form of presentation was aimed at mak-ing a dramatic case for Christian freedom, the book still jolts one's thinking. It is not an easy concept to accept.

One of the most significant sections for me was the call

for realism. Ellul feels that Christians tend to lack realism more than good intentions and noble ideals. Realism helps us see that violence operates within certain laws. Violence begets violence—nothing else. It's a delusion to think that with just a little violence I'll be able to bring about peace and harmony. There is a "sameness" to violence. Propaganda is propaganda, whether it is used by a ruthless tyrant or a national church body. Violence always tries to justify itself. Violence is so abhorrent when seen clearly that rationalizations and justifications are used to mask the reality.

Ellul calls one to live in the world as it is, not as how one wishes it might be. With that kind of realism, he still calls for the possibility of nonviolence as an alternative to the way the world generally functions.

The key theological issue for me in these times between the times is the theology of the cross. Some non-Lutherans have been of great help in new awareness of how the cross speaks to a lifestyle of faith.

James Douglass, A Roman Catholic layman, is the author of *The Non-Violent Cross.* It was a privilege to spend the afternoon with him today. I was grateful that it was just a small group and informal. That's a better atmosphere for learning to know one another.

Jim senses such power in the cross. He sees hope only if we recognize that the future belongs to a different kind of power than weapons technology. He is convinced of the emerging power of those without any weapon except the one weapon available to those on the margins of life —suffering for truth and justice.

I have a feeling Ed will be one of those rare persons

whose friendship will continue to influence my life. His lifestyle challenges me in a helpful way. He has the rare quality of being able to live out a voluntary poverty and a radical nonviolence without putting you down if your understanding and style differs from his. When you are with him, you experience gospel, not law. Yet there is no hint of "cheap grace," no toning down the hard gospel of the cross.

Ed suggests I do some reading in Thomas Merton, the Trappist monk who has had a great deal of influence in his life.

One of the qualities needed for the '70s is "staying power." There is a feeling that the '60s had much that was fad. People dabbled in certain movements but tended to lose interest or become bored.

The most impressive groups are the ones with a deep commitment that doesn't give up when the faddists quit. The Quakers and the Mennonites have been working for peace when it was a popular movement and also when it was the most unpopular message.

To follow the signals of nonviolence may mean changing our way of life. I am tempted to quit my present work and simply devote time to the question—assuming that somehow we'd find a way to support ourselves as a family. Tempted is not quite the right word. I feel "called" in a way that hasn't happened often in my life. A wise church father once told a young pastor, "When God opens a door, you are to walk through it. Just make sure you don't start opening the doors ahead of you and thinking God is doing it."

The question is always there for me: who is opening this door?

None of the Above

Lanza Del Vasto is certainly one of the fascinating figures of our day. He has been very helpful to me through his writings. I felt I knew him after reading his autobiographical account in *Return to the Source.* I am glad more of his works are being published in English.

In the opening chapter of *Warriors of Peace,* Del Vasto gives a helpful description of nonviolence. One can speak of nonviolence only in the context of conflict. One cannot call someone nonviolent who tries to preserve his own safety when the world about him is in strife. The man who leads a sheltered life is perhaps nonviolent but it is impossible to tell. But in the situation of conflict, if one responds to violence without resorting to violence, then one can begin to use the term nonviolence with meaning.

Del Vasto indicates that there are four possible attitudes

which come to mind when one thinks of responses to violence.

1. *Fight:* rush in to give as we get, and twice as much if we are able.

2. *Flight:* take to our heels and run for cover.

3. *Neutrality:* don't get involved, it's none of our business.

4. *Capitulation:* give in, surrender, work for a compromise.

But there is a fifth alternative, and that's what Jesus was pointing to in the Sermon on the Mount. The fifth alternative is what is often called nonviolence. The key thing to understand is that nonviolence *excludes* the other four. This is especially important when people think of it as some combination of neutrality, surrender, or running away. Nonviolence not only excludes fighting, it also excludes the cowardice of giving in or of not being involved at all.

It seems so appropriate in this age of computer forms and quick checklists that one way of thinking of nonviolence is to check that last possibility usually designated "none of the above." To choose none of the options commonly accepted seems more consistent with the gospel. Jesus offers us a new choice, an alternative lifestyle, a call to be a peculiar people as we begin to understand his life and teachings.

You have heard that it was said, "An eye for an eye and a tooth for a tooth." But I say to you, Do not resist one who is evil. But if any one strikes you on the right cheek, turn to him the other also; and if any one would sue you and take your coat, let him have your cloak as well; and if any one forces you to go one mile, go with him two miles. Give to him who begs from you, and do not refuse him who would borrow from you.

MATT. 5:38-42

We really don't know how to handle this quotation. We have a picture of Jesus putting the high-jump bar above our ability to clear it, but at least we'll keep trying. That's the purpose of this lofty idealism. I have never yet met a fundamentalist or literalist who doesn't hedge on Matthew 5:39. "Do not resist one who is evil." We do everything except take seriously this portion of Scripture. Yet this is at the heart of the New Testament message. The intent of this passage is reconciliation. We *will* have enemies! We are not to be concerned with defeating them, but rather with changing the relationship which puts us into conflict.

Thaddeus Stevens was a member of the cabinet when Abraham Lincoln was president. As the cabinet was discussing the treatment of people in the South after the Civil War, Mr. Stevens shouted, "Enemies are to be destroyed!" Abraham Lincoln quietly responded, "Mr. Stevens, do not I destroy my enemy when I make him my friend?"

We keep insisting that the radical life called for in the Sermon on the Mount is not realistic. For the most part, we determine that intellectually, and therefore never try it. It's encouraging to hear the witness of those who have accepted it as a way of life.

Lanza Del Vasto is the founder of a Christian community, the Society of the Ark, committed to a life of nonviolence. On one occasion they had a visitor who stayed for a week and received the gracious hospitality of the community, a hospitality extended to many strangers throughout the year. This particular guest helped himself to a few of the community's possessions when he left. The community gathered together and reached consensus on a course of action. By piecing together parts of a letter from scraps of paper left in the stranger's room, they had some idea of his destination when he fled. One of the members of the Society of the Ark went into Paris and located the man.

"I've come from the community to reassure you that we are happy to have been of service to you," he began. There was the offer of further help if needed and also a gentle invitation into a changed lifestyle.

The Society of the Ark had no further contact with the man. They never learned whether the man's life was changed, but their course of action flowed from the community's understanding of the teachings of Jesus.

Nonviolence is still considered by many to be naive in the face of the realities of the world situation. The questions come in the same words almost everywhere one discusses nonviolence: "It worked for Gandhi because he was dealing with Great Britain, and for Martin Luther King because he was dealing with the United States government, but it never would have succeeded against Adolf Hitler."

These comments still bother me, not so much in the academic sense of being challenged by a group and expected to come up with an answer, but in how much I am committed to nonviolence or the way of the cross.

When Daniel Berrigan lectured on nonviolence and the Sermon on the Mount, someone accused him of being naive and said, "Father, no one can live the way you outlined. Do you know what will happen if you try? Do you know where your advice will lead someone?" Father Berrigan responded, "Yes, I know where it leads. Before you start down this path you better make sure you look good on wood."

Arguments against nonviolence don't shake me as much as they used to. It is quite clear that violent answers solve nothing. We have been trying to solve the world's problems through force, bombs, and threats. These ways have not worked. We don't know if nonviolence could work on a large scale because it has never been tried as the political philosophy for international relations. I don't see how it could be anymore expensive than the present arms race.

What is this nonviolent method that offers new hope? Its simplest and most obvious statement is found in the religious literature of many faiths, most familiarly to Christians in the Sermon on the Mount. At its heart, it is the effort to maintain unity among men. It seeks to knit the break in the sense of community whose fracture is both a cause and a result of human conflict. It relies upon love rather than hate, and though it involves a willingness to accept rather than inflict suffering, it is neither passive nor cowardly. It offers a way of meeting evil without relying on the ability to cause pain to the human being through whom evil is expressed. It seeks to change the attitude of the opponent rather than to force his submission through violence. It is, in short, the practical effort to overcome evil with good. . . . We believe it is practical, and poli-

tically relevant, for men and women to move the world toward peace by individually practicing peace themselves, here and now.

FROM A QUAKER STATEMENT

Christianity has in the long run limited violence far less than violence has limited Christianity.

JAMES DOUGLASS

It is a great disservice to give people the idea that to be truly Christian we must renounce power and become powerless people. Nothing could be farther from the truth. Rollo May states so clearly that power does not result in violence. Rather violence springs as a noncreative reaction to a feeling of impotence.

Power in its root meaning simply means "to be able." Any productive and fulfilling life must flow from this "capability." Jesus promised us power with the coming of the Holy Spirit. This gift is still promised, and to reject power is to reject God's gift and intention for us.

The unique Christian insight comes at the point of the definition and understanding of power. The world pictures force, brute strength, money, muscle, tanks, bombs, tyranny, monopolies—the list goes on and on. The Christian pictures the cross. In the "foolishness" of this symbol of power the Christian senses a radically different kind of power. It is a new way of being "capable." A picture of this different definition would be Jesus standing in front of Pilate. Pilate represents all the power of the great empire of Rome. Jesus appears to be one lonely, solitary, impotent man. It is clear through the eye of faith, however, that the real power is incarnate in the solitary figure.

Nonviolence is often misunderstood as impotence. On

the contrary, it is the epitome of power. It does, however, understand power quite differently from a world caught up in the worship of force.

It is so difficult for the negative term, nonviolence, to convey the positive power inherent in the concept. One senses why Gandhi coined a phrase, *satyagraha,* rather than using the word for nonviolence in his own language. Even though I'm not sure I understand *satyagraha* (the definition is *truth power* or *soul power*) at least it is clear that we are talking about something more than the absence of violence.

Nonviolence is not a cover for cowardice, but it is the supreme virtue of the brave. . . . Cowardice is wholly inconsistent with nonviolence.

GANDHI

The real stories seldom make the media. We were kept informed of facts during the civil rights movement, of descriptions of the acts of protest, but I doubt if readers and viewers got a real sense of the power of nonviolence. The power was in the hearts of the participants.

David was then a young man, a devout Quaker and one for whom nonviolence was a way of life, not a political tactic. He and a black friend went into a drugstore in the Deep South and calmly ordered cokes. In retrospect, those "sit-ins" seem so harmless a protest, but at the time this was done, the action was explosive. David related that he felt a sharp object jabbing into his back. He turned to look into the angriest eyes he had ever seen. The eyes sparked with hate. Now that he had turned, the sharp knife was aimed directly at his heart.

35

David looked directly into the eyes of his adversary. He spoke softly and calmly. "Friend," he said, (And he meant that. One misses the whole power of nonviolence if he thinks that was said sarcastically.) "Friend, whether you push that knife into my heart or not is obviously up to you. I want you to know that in either event, I love you."

The man's hand trembled a little, the knife fell to the floor and he almost ran from the drugstore. He had been confronted with a power he had never experienced before. He didn't or couldn't understand this form of power, but make no mistake, it is power!

Nonviolence is not a garment to be put off and on at will. Its seat is in the heart, and it must be an inseparable part of our very being. . . .

It is better to be violent, if there is violence in our hearts, than to put on the cloak of nonviolence to cover impotence. Violence is any day preferable to impotence. There is hope for a violent man to become nonviolent. There is no hope for the impotent.

GANDHI

The discussion period after a lecture is almost always more helpful than the lecture itself.

In response to a presentation on nonviolence there were a number of "Yes, but" reactions:

"But you might get hurt." It should be clear that the disciple of nonviolence must be ready to suffer or even die. Just as the recruiting officer cannot promise that one won't get hurt in the armed conflict, so the advocate of nonviolent resistance must acknowledge that injury and suffering are certainly possible. The difference comes at

the point where violent actions hope to make the opponent suffer the most until he surrenders, while nonviolence stresses redemptive suffering. This means breaking the power of the enemy by absorbing the suffering inflicted by him without retaliation in kind or spirit.

"But it's not natural for me to think that way." Any realistic call for nonviolence assumes a training process and the development of strong disciplines. This training is not only in tactics but also in the spiritual and philosophical roots of one's being. It is necessary to develop a new way of thinking and new habits, not only to devise new strategies.

"But you're just giving us another more subtle method of getting your way." There is no denial that nonviolent action is a form of power. For those who understand it as passivity, there is a need to clarify that it is an active powerful force. But it is not a subtle manipulation to get one's own way. Nonviolence does not mean that I'll be proved right, but rather that truth will ultimately prevail.

"But the civil rights movement was *violent because the white oppressors really did suffer."* Nonviolent action does indeed bring social dislocation and change! When a group has derived its comfort and way of life from oppressing another group, they will experience much discomfort when that situation is changed. In violent revolution, the intent would be to throw off the enemy by force and perhaps through killing. Nonviolence seeks to change the situation without destroying the enemy. Even though he may experience pain, the oppressor is not really free until he is no longer the oppressor.

When the church talks about nonviolence we already have our symbol—the cross. It isn't as though we are now confronted with a strange new concept, we are really challenged to take a new look at the meaning of the cross. It is the symbol for an understanding of power which the world has never understood.

The doctrine of the cross is sheer folly to those on their way to ruin, but to us who are on the way to salvation it is the power of God. Scripture says, "I will destroy the wisdom of the wise, and bring to nothing the cleverness of the clever." Where is your wise man now, your man of learning, or your subtle debater—limited, all of them, to this passing age? God has made the wisdom of this world look foolish. As God in his wisdom ordained, the world failed to find him by its wisdom, and he chose to save those who have faith by the folly of the Gospel. Jews call for miracles, Greeks look for wisdom; but we proclaim Christ—yes, Christ nailed to the cross; and though this is a stumbling block to Jews and folly to Greeks, yet to those who have heard his call, Jews and Greeks alike, he is the power of God and the wisdom of God.

Divine folly is wiser than the wisdom of man, and divine weakness stronger than man's strength. My brothers, think what sort of people you are, whom God has called. Few of you are men of wisdom, by any human standard; few are powerful or highly born. Yet, to shame the wise, God has chosen what the world counts folly, and to shame what is strong, God has chosen what the world counts weakness. He has chosen things low and contemptible, mere nothings, to overthrow the existing order.

1 COR. 1:18-28 NEB

John Howard Yoder is a Mennonite biblical scholar. His writings have moved me deeply, and I think will continue to have an effect upon my thinking and my life. He is especially challenging in regard to the theology of the cross. His *Politics of Jesus* centers on the cross and forces the reader to confront that event. For Yoder, the cross is not only a prescribed instrument of propitiation, but also a political alternative to both insurrection and quietism. Jesus spoke of the cross in a meaningful way before he died on one. He spoke not only of his own death in the future but of the cross itself as symbol. Disciples are to take up their cross and follow him. This must have had clear meaning to those who heard these words. Yoder's premise is that the cross has always meant the price of social nonconformity, and the believer's cross still means that today.

A provocative question at the church convention went unnoticed today. At least no one else I've talked with seems to have heard it or thought it very profound.

The youth of the church, when asked to give their report, did so by having half a dozen young people at various floor microphones asking questions, making affirmations, and releasing helium-filled balloons. Most of the delegates seem to have accepted this brief five minutes as a diversion from convention business.

It's unfortunate for the church that we didn't hear that one brief question from floor microphone number three. "If we are the church of Jesus Christ and followers of his way, how come we haven't had any of our bishops go to jail?"

One of the best things about Holden Village is the remarkable mix of people. We feel a genuine sense of community in such a short time and it's not because all the people agree or think alike. There is a Spirit at work. Today I felt that Spirit in my conversation with a man who is struggling with his anger.

The lecture had been on nonviolence, and there was a good discussion period following. One man stayed after everyone had gone and shared with me his desire to live out the gospel of love, but the Native Americans who lived on the reservation near his home kept stealing gasoline from the tank in his farm yard. He had installed a lock but it had been broken off. Next he had installed a spot light to prevent them from coming at night, but the stealing continued.

He was an honest struggler with the gospel and I liked him. It isn't often that I prescribe a particular course of action, but in the context of our conversation it seemed appropriate. I said, "If I understand the gospel, it says that you take off the lock and put up a sign that says 'Help Yourself If You Need Gasoline!' I guess I'd leave the spotlight on so that if anyone comes at night they could read the sign."

There was a mixture of anguish and excitement in his face. His response surprised me. He said, "Oh, would that be freedom to be able to do that and have the awful burden of protecting that gas tank off my mind!"

He understood the gospel. It isn't a new law, it's a freedom. I don't know what he did when he went back home. He will never know what he did for me. I was almost kidding when I suggested the solution, and he accepted it with such grace. He understood more than I said.

I have learned that an age in which politicians talk

*about peace is an age in which everybody expects war;
the great men of the earth would not talk of peace so
much if they did not secretly believe it possible, with*
one more war, *to annihilate their enemies forever.*

THOMAS MERTON

People have such a great need to label other people. To
attach a label is more important than to listen to what
someone is saying. I shared a pastoral conference platform
today with a fellow minister, and we tried to present
some of our concerns about the role of the church in
waging peace. Some in the audience seemed fearful we
were pacifists, and their questions were related to this
rather than focusing on what we had said. When pressed
this way I tend to respond that I'm almost a pacifist. I
think it would have been more helpful to refuse to answer
any labeling question and just quote Roland Bainton:
"The world needs peace more than it needs pacifists."

John Howard Yoder has done a great service in writing
his book *Nevertheless*. In it he describes 25 types of pacifism. This makes it clear that there is no single position
which can be labeled pacifism.

For me, pacifism has always meant some form of withdrawal from the world and from difficult struggles. Yoder
challenges my definition by rejecting any withdrawal from
the world. I also tend to think of pacifists as holding a
naive optimism about the inherent goodness of man.
Again, Yoder rejects this assumption, and I am forced to
deal seriously with his articulation of a thoroughly biblical
understanding of the nature of man and yet a commitment to a pacifist position.

41

If I am inclined to any form of pacifism, it is Yoder's "pacifism of the messianic community." As I understand it, this pacifism has five basic themes:

1. *Jesus as Lord.* Other forms of pacifism have Christian adherents, but for Yoder the person and work of Jesus Christ provides the foundation for his pacifism and Jesus' resurrection provides the enablement. Where other theologians make Jesus the norm in creed and thought, Yoder sees him as the norm for political humanity—for the way one lives in a social, economic, political sense, as well as our spiritual life.

2. *Centrality of the Cross.* The power of the cross is the alternative to both violent revolution and a withdrawal from the social and political issues of the world.

3. *Human Community.* One individual can crystalize widespread awareness of a problem or can elicit great admiration, but only a continuing community dedicated to a deviant value system can change the world. Besides, it is a rare individual who can stand and make a solitary witness. Most of us need the support system of other people who share our faith and life. Most of us need the communion of saints.

4. *Realism.* Hope is not based on the inherent goodness of man. The key for Yoder is the kingdom of God with some new criterion for what is possible. His optimism is not based upon what is humanly feasible.

5. *Consistent Nonviolence.* Pacifism is not simply an attitude toward the issue of war and peace but is the style for all of life.

We need to expand our awareness of violence and violent systems. I realized this at the last two retreats when

I asked the participants to free associate with the word "violent."

No one mentioned political rhetoric, high birth and death rates in many countries, manipulation, fraud, gossip, unemployment, nonparticipation in decisions affecting one's life, the draft, calling a child stupid, non-communication, withholding love, the whole rich/poor division.

And I would add another form of violence—the major part of our educational system. Why should it be that 90% of five year old children measure a "high creativity" level, and by the age of seven the number who measure "highly creative" has dropped to 10%?

When he called his society together Jesus gave its members a new way of life to live. He gave them a new way to deal with offenders—by forgiving them. He gave them a new way to deal with violence—by suffering. He gave them a new way to deal with money—by sharing it. He gave them a new way to deal with the problems of leadership—by drawing upon the gift of every member, even the most humble. He gave them a new way to deal with a corrupt society—by building a new order, not smashing the old. He gave them a new pattern of relationships between man and woman, between parent and child, between master and slave, in which was made concrete a radical new vision of what it means to be a human person. He gave them a new attitude toward the state and toward the "enemy nation."

JOHN HOWARD YODER

For all the talk about nonviolence, Gandhi pointedly reminds us that nonviolence cannot be preached. It has to be practiced.

43

Fat Sheep,
Lean Sheep

If you want peace, work for justice.

POPE PAUL VI

A large, round table sits in the middle of the room, attractively set for a dinner party. Sixteen guests arrive and seat themselves around the table. Conversation diminishes as the host appears with a vast array of food he has prepared for the pleasure of his hungry guests. Everyone smiles as they see the steaming food and cold, crisp salads. Stomachs groan as the sixteen people smell the aroma of the meats and fish, fruits and vegetables.

One guest, obviously much wealthier than the others, reaches out and takes half the food for himself. He samples each dish, leaving much uneaten on his plate. When he has eaten his fill, he yawns, stretches, and rubs his bulging abdomen. He lights a cigar, sips his coffee, and seems oblivious to the fact that the rest of the guests must be content to share the remaining food. Some receive a portion that will leave them inadequately nourished, and some will get no food at all.

Americans are six percent of the world's population and we consume nearly half the world's food supply. Is it that we fail to see the others sitting at the world's table? Or do we consciously choose such inequity?

As for you, my flock, thus says the Lord God: Behold, I judge between sheep and sheep, rams and he-goats. Is it not enough for you to feed on the good pasture, that you must tread down with your feet the rest of your pasture; and to drink clear water, that you must foul the rest with your feet? And must my sheep eat what you have trodden down with your feet, and drink what you have fouled with your feet?

Therefore, thus says the Lord God to them: Behold, I, I myself will judge between the fat sheep and the lean sheep. Because you push with side and shoulder and thrust at all the weak with your horns, till you have scattered them abroad, I will save my flock, they shall no longer be a prey; and I will judge between sheep and sheep."

EZEKIEL 34:17-22

Today 30,000 people somewhere in the world will die from starvation. Two-thirds of our global family will go to bed hungry tonight, while most Americans are over-fed, over-weight, potential members of Weight-watchers and TOPS clubs. We exert a disproportionate demand on the world's food supply. We do this because we are rich. We can afford to buy what we want, when we want it.

Be merciful to your fat sheep, Lord.

Wednesday night: Why do the boys always seem to choose this night to make a big batch of popcorn? I think it's a conspiracy. I'm really hungry, and unless I keep very busy during the day or go to bed fairly early, I seem to spend an inordinate amount of time thinking about my stomach.

Wednesday has been a "fast day" for me during the past eight months. Being rather undisciplined, I find it a difficult commitment to keep. I didn't know I was so food oriented. Mark challenges these "fast days" with all the fervor a 17-year-old, 6′ 3″ teen-ager with two hollow legs can muster. His questions are good ones, and I have to tell him I'm not completely clear in my own mind why I think it's important for me.

"Does it really do anyone any good?" he asks. "Is it just to make *you* feel good? What dent is it going to make in the world hunger problem? Why shouldn't we eat when there is so much food around us?"

I'm tempted to agree that the gesture of not eating can be a shallow one—something like the women of the church deciding to give up dessert at their circle meeting. And yet nothing gets done if some small first step isn't taken. I can certainly rationalize that since my not eating doesn't put food in the mouths of starving children, why deny myself the pleasure of meals on Wednesday? Kathy leaves lima beans on her plate because they taste "stuffy" and defies me with a look that communicates, "Wrap them up and send them to India if you can, but I'm not going to eat them!"

My hope for Wednesdays is that I will begin to think less about myself and more about others, beginning with those around me. I am certainly more aware of how it must feel to be hungry. I think of children who cry them-

47

selves to sleep and the utter agony of a mother who cannot give them the milk they need. I remember these wretched of the earth and ask God to put his arms around them. The money I save from going without meals is put in a special fund and sent to Lutheran World Relief, World Vision, Bread for the World, CARE or some other organization fighting world hunger.

Deep down inside of me—heart or stomach, I'm not sure—I feel the excessive consumption of food has to stop with me. I have to say *no*. It means not only that I look at my eating habits on Wednesday, but each day I must be more aware of the need to change the consumption patterns I have been taking for granted.

Another dimension to fasting one day a week is that I feel a sense of community with other persons who are fasting. Some of these people are members of a loosely knit organization called the Order of St. Martin. Bill White, a member of this group, has made some helpful comments regarding fasting:

Fasting is more than not eating. Not eating is a physical process; fasting involves the total person. A decision not to eat often begins with determination, but a fast requires preparation. For me, this preparation consists of focusing on someone or something. As I think, pray, and anticipate, I begin to identify with other persons, an identification that heightens as the fast progresses.

I have fasted as a way of concentrating on hunger, or oppression in general, or something more specific, such as the victims of the bombing in Vietnam. When a friend was arrested for violating the Selective Service Act,

I fasted until I could greet him in jail. When we came together, there was a real meeting.

In the Old Testament, people were urged to fast to identify with others—particularly the poor and the oppressed. A person who fasted, or emptied him/herself identified with the afflicted. Thus the fast became an act of repentance.

Fasting, like all aspects of the life of faith, can be used as a means of deception and spiritual one-upmanship. It can be turned into a work. It was phoney fasting that provoked Isaiah to shout, "Fasting means to break the bonds of injustice, to loosen the yoke of the oppressed, to share your bread with the hungry, to cover the naked, to house the homeless!"

In summary, fasting without peacemaking is a lie.

During my reading tonight I was moved by an incident recorded by Maria de Jesus, a Brazilian slum dweller in her diary, *Child of the Dark:*

When I got out of bed, Vera was already awake and she asked me:

"Mama, isn't today my birthday?"

"It is. My congratulations. I wish you happiness."

"Are you going to make a cake for me?"

"I don't know. If I can get some money. . . ." I lit the fire and went to carry water. The women were complaining that the water was running out slow.

The garbagemen have gone by. I got little paper. I went by the factory to pick up some rags. I began to feel dizzy. I made up my mind to go to Dona Angelina's house to ask for a little coffee. Dona Angelina gave me some. When I went out I told her I was feeling better.

"It's hunger. You need to eat!"

49

"But what I earn isn't enough." I have lost eight kilos. I have no meat on my bones, and the little I did have has gone. I picked up the papers and went out. When I went past a shop window I saw my reflection. I looked the other way because I thought I was seeing a ghost.

I fried fish and made some corn mush for the children to eat with the fish. When Vera showed up and saw the mush inside the pot she asked:

"Is that a cake? Today is my birthday!"

"No, it isn't cake. It's mush."

"I don't like mush!"

I got some milk. I gave her milk and mush. She ate it, sobbing. Who am I to make a cake?

The Washington, D.C. contingent of the Order of St. Martin—a group concerned with peace and global justice —tells us they had a progressive non-dinner on Monday night. Guests were invited to the first home for a non-appetizer and concluded the evening at Nyla and Larry's for a non-dessert. World hunger was the topic of the evening's conversation and the money saved for the progressive non-meal was forwarded to Lutheran World Relief.

For anyone who eats and drinks without discerning the body, eats and drinks judgment upon himself.

1 Cor. 11:29

This is the scripture that kept me trembling as I took my first communion. I did not want to be an "unworthy" guest.

Now I wonder, could not discerning the "body" refer to the Body of Christ—the vast number of Christian brothers and sisters throughout the world who are hun-

gry or in need of liberation? When I commune without
even being aware that they are suffering and in need of
my love and compassion, do I not eat and drink un-
worthily?

*Again I saw all the oppressions that are practiced under
the sun. And behold, the tears of the oppressed, and
they had no one to comfort them! On the side of their
oppressors there was power, and there was no one to
comfort them. And I thought the dead who are already
dead more fortunate than the living who are still alive;
but better than both is he who has not yet been, and has
not seen the evil deeds that are done under the sun.*

Eccles. 4:1-3

A frank and compelling article in one of the last issues
of *Event* magazine was in the form of an open letter to
church leaders from a group of Christian missionaries in
Chile. The letter began:

*Greetings in our Lord Jesus Christ. We are writing to
you out of a common concern for the one gospel we both
profess, and the one kingdom of justice, equality and
peace to which we are both committed.*

They wrote with passion about the awakening social
consciousness in Chile and discovering the liberating presence of the Lord. What angered and pained them was to
see such contradictions between the gospel and the actions of the United States:

*While we realize that the problems of dehumanization
and poverty are many and complex, we write to you
about capitalism and the one aspect of it which we consider pivotal in causing suffering and oppression in Chile
and Latin America—overseas investment.*

The missionaries explained how they saw our foreign policy, foreign aid, and our political stance as being one which protected U.S. private investment. The economics of the poorer nations are dominated by the rich nations for their own profit without concern for the dehumanizing effect and untold suffering of those at the mercy of the capitalistic system.

When political and economic pressure by the U.S. fails to secure "pro-American" (i.e. pro-U.S. business) behavior on the part of Third World nations, military intervention is often resorted to, as it was in Guatemala, Cuba, and the Dominican Republic.

One paragraph stood out as I reread the article:

The position of the church before this reality can no longer be an ambiguous one. The position of Christ was in no way ambiguous; his was an option for the poor and against anyone or any system that stood in the way of man's liberation. The present international economic system is a situation of sin, and as such it must be rejected. It is not enough for the churches to elaborate theologies and declarations of concern for the poor. If Christians do not effectively opt for the poor and the oppressed by entering into their struggle, then the church cannot really claim to be a sign of the liberating presence of Christ in the world.

"The Spirit of the Lord is upon me because he has anointed me to preach good news to the poor. He has sent me to proclaim release to the captives and recovering of sight to the blind, to set at liberty those who are oppressed, to proclaim the acceptable year of the Lord."

Luke 4:18-19

A conference on liberation theology was held in Detroit this month. Liberation theology is not new, but most of us in America have paid little attention to it. Since the conference made the religion section of *Time* magazine, we will probably begin to discuss it now.

Most people, hearing about liberation theology, will label it "communist" and can therefore dismiss it. We will get defensive about the anti-capitalistic language and the indictment of us as wealthy oppressors.

Actually the language at Detroit was no more revolutionary than that which we have been singing at vespers for centuries:

My soul doth magnify the Lord,
and my spirit hath rejoiced in God my Savior.
For he hath regarded
the low estate of his handmaiden.
For behold from henceforth
all generations shall call me blessed.
For he that is mighty hath done to me great things;
And holy is his Name.
And his mercy is on them that fear him
from generation to generation.
He hath showed strength with his arm;
he hath scattered the proud in the imagination of their
*   hearts.*
He hath put down the mighty from their seats,
and exalted them of low degree.
He hath filled the hungry with good things;
and the rich he hath sent empty away.

It is difficult to live with the knowledge that we are oppressors. As Joe Barndt says, we are the Egyptians in the Exodus story. The chaplains in Pharaoh's court have a difficult time speaking a prophetic word.

In the *Mission on Six Continents* film, one of the memorable comments was made by Manas Buthelezi. This gentle man from South Africa, theologian, scholar, and champion of oppressed people, wonders how our churches and we Christian people can speak out against the "system" and the values of our Western society when we are so much a part of it.

Exploitation of fellow human beings is for us such an accepted thing, we scarcely realize we are guilty. I never ask myself who may be the recipient of injustice when I purchase inexpensive rubber thongs from Taiwan, paneling for our house from Korea, spices from the Caribbean. I try to forget when I purchase sugar that perhaps it was grown on the only tillable land in Haiti, where starvation is a fact of life.

Perhaps God does not hold me accountable for those areas of which I am ignorant or do not understand, but I am accountable for responding to areas of concern which I cannot possibly misunderstand: refusing to patronize petroleum companies where I know their policies foster conditions of degradation in Africa or South America; support for the migrant workers.

My prayer is that guilt be replaced with compassion, that ignorance become understanding, and the struggles of the oppressed become my struggle.

I sit on a man's back choking him and making him carry me, and yet assure myself and others that I am sorry for him and wish to lighten his load by all possible means —except by getting off his back.

LEO TOLSTOY

*The innocents of the world suffer, just as the Son
suffered, because every living man makes them suffer. It
is man's responsibility, in and through the cross of the
Son, to see that the innocents stop suffering. Man either
gives life by himself taking on their suffering in that community of Christ working toward a new earth or he mur-
ders by turning from the God in man to the idolatry of
a distant deity. There is only one God, and he has become
man. Man can possess no life in God apart from God's
life in the Suffering Servant.*

JAMES DOUGLASS

It is refreshing to note in E. F. Schumacher's book,
Small Is Beautiful, that so renowned an economist is
saying the system of production that ravishes nature and
mutilates man needs to be changed. There are higher priorities and motivations than "Is it economical?" We are
using capital (irreplacable primary resources) as if it were
income.

The United States is not over-populated. We have 57
people per square mile, compared with the average of
70 people per square mile worldwide. Our land is en-
dowed with an abundance of rich natural resources. Yet,
like some giant octopus, we reach out into other parts
of the world and in so doing claim for ourselves 40%
of the world's resources. In order for us to continue to
live in the manner in which we have grown accustomed,
we must do this, because our industrial system cannot survive on our internal resources.

The world and its resources have been entrusted to all
of God's children for the benefit of all. I believe this.
I also believe this must have some bearing on my lifestyle.

55

It was interesting to hear Marge Wold comment on a tape that the Old Testament concept of *shalom* was not one of psychological well-being—that is, not the idea that somehow you will be free from distress and turmoil—but one of material well-being, of security and personal safety. The Hebrew greeting "Is it *shalom* with you?" meant, "Have you got enough cash today?"

Where but in North America or Europe would I dare to ask, "Is it *shalom* with you today?"

I suggest that we are thieves in a way. If I take anything that I do not need for my own immediate use, and keep it, I thieve it from somebody else. . . . In India we have three millions of people having to be satisfied with one meal a day, and that meal consisting of unleavened bread containing no fat in it and a pinch of salt. You and I have no right to anything that we really have until these three millions are clothed and better fed. You and I, who ought to know better, must adjust our wants and even undergo voluntary starvation in order that they may be nursed, fed and clothed.

GANDHI

At the conference today Joe Barndt said, "Let's not forget that when we talk redistribution of goods here in the United States, we are really talking about the redistribution of stolen goods."

We have a hard time living with a global perspective. I guess it's because it frightens us, and we instinctively feel our life style would have to change radically.

He who closes his ear to the cry of the poor will himself cry out and not be heard.

PROV. 21:13

It was my turn to talk with the Holden Village community today. The schedule tacked up on the bulletin board under the tree simply listed "Namibia" as the topic for the 10 o'clock discussion.

Only two of the fifty people present had ever heard of Namibia. They were aware it was a country in southwest Africa. No one was aware that Namibia has the dubious distinction of being the world's most exploited country.

This country, about the size of Montana, having some of the richest copper and diamond mines in the world, is a good example of our need for global concern. The country is 87% black and most of these people are Christian, in fact the majority are Lutherans. Living under the illegal, oppressive thumb of the government of South Africa, these fellow Christians have responded to decades of oppression under the *apartheid* system (strict separation of black and white citizens for the benefit of the white population) with nonviolence.

Blacks, divided by tribes, are forced to live on reservations called bantustans and need bulky passbooks to move about anywhere in Namibia. Men who sign up for work are classified according to strength and sent to work in the copper mines for 6 to 12 months without being allowed to see their families. Blacks are denied the right to vote, to own property, to associate in public places with whites. They have few schools to which they can send their children. They can be arrested and jailed for the slightest infraction of the law—or for no reason whatsoever. If a man marries outside his own bantustan, he cannot legally live with his wife.

American corporations have partial or complete control of many copper mines and available oil. These American corporations have participated in the whole system of *apartheid* so as to be able to hire cheap labor and not "upset the government of South Africa."

In 1971 one of the Lutheran bishops of Namibia, Leonard Auala, defied the government of South Africa, writing a strong letter of protest saying his people could no longer tolerate the inhumane treatment they were receiving. The stand of the bishop and other church leaders precipitated the first strike of black workers and almost brought to a halt the production of copper for over a year. Few positive results, however, occurred because of this strike. It was a beginning—a spark that shed some light on what had seemed like a hopeless situation for the Namibians.

Pressure has continually been brought to bear on the South African government through the United Nations, Lutheran World Federation, the World Council of Churches, and church and political organizations within Namibia itself. Some changes are slowly occurring, but one wonders how long these people can respond nonviolently to the oppression.

My point as I talked was this. Once again, we have an example of our country putting economic values and greed before human values. Church leaders in Namibia have pleaded with our country and others to stop stripping their country of its natural resources. If and when independence does come, the land will have become a barren wasteland, unable to support its inhabitants.

The Namibians are learning, and perhaps we, too, will learn what Gandhi meant when he said, "The first principle of nonviolent action is that of non-cooperation with everything humiliating."

When I try to clarify what I value, Christ's gift of freedom ranks high on my priority list. With a growing understanding that oppressors need liberation as well as the oppressed, I realize how urgently we must work for justice. Dr. Martin Luther King understood that the white man needed liberation as well as the black. The biblical concept of *shalom* implies a wholeness, a completeness, a bringing together of something shattered.

Can there be *shalom* when even one brother/sister is suffering and there is no reconciliation?

But now in Christ Jesus you who once were far off have been brought near in the blood of Christ. For he is our peace, who has made us both one, and has broken down the dividing wall of hostility, by abolishing in his flesh the law of commandments and ordinances, that he might create in himself one new man in place of the two, so making peace, and might reconcile us both to God in one body through the cross, thus bringing hostility to an end.
EPH. 2:13-16

This weekend we served as resource persons at a family retreat for a small Lutheran congregation. It was very refreshing for us to share the time with them. They call themselves a family and we could sense the truth of the term. They welcomed us into that family quickly and genuinely.

In the midst of the fun, relaxation, and fellowship, we were to make several presentations. The one which seemed to get the most resistance was a discussion of global consciousness. People felt we had problems with our own guilt and were attempting to lay some of it on them.

How do we confront the reality of injustice in the world and our role in it without ending in a paralyzing guilt trip? It seems so difficult to present the challenge of the gospel without toning it down and yet without changing it into a new law. Apparently we were not able to convey that *we* will not be free until we are no longer oppressors. It is hard to see our lifestyle of comfort as a problem.

The revolutionary is the man of conscience in today's world. There is and can be no other man of conscience today, for the world as man has thus organized it, socially and economically—as distinct from its created forms and life—is intolerable. To tolerate the morally intolerable is gradually to lose life, as man who lets the water close above him; to fail to see the intolerable, as most do, is to live in less than the world, and for less than man. . . . What begins as a recognition of massive injustice must grow into a commitment to global love. Thus the man of conscience faces the world today as a revolutionary seized by the crisis of injustice, and thus he prepares to act in it.
JAMES DOUGLASS

Search
for the Simple Life

The mail today brought a news release quoting Dr. Carl Mau, general secretary of Lutheran World Federation. Dr. Mau urges a "voluntary austerity" and asked that Christians "erect powerful signs of a new simplicity in life style."

What kind of "powerful signs" do we need to erect for the world to see? Those who attempt to live a simple life will certainly challenge our American value system and the basic rules of our Western industrial society. Simple life is a blow to materialism and consumerism, but it is certainly much more than doing without luxuries, convenience foods, and a new car.

Perhaps if we attempt to lead a simple life, we will have a clearer understanding of what Jesus meant when he said, "I came that you might have life and have it abundantly." I have always thought of simple life as the opposite of abundant life. Perhaps that has been part of the problem for me.

"Simple: an adjective meaning not compound, not complicated, elaborate or highly involved. Unsophisticated, plain, frank, natural, humble and unpretentious."

I note the dictionary doesn't say simple means *easy,* nor does it use *convenient* as a synonym. My attempts at simplifying life are met with frustration, much planning, and "making do." I fear that, like many people I know, I worship the god called *convenience.* This is a tempting god because I find very appealing its promises of "a quicker way," more leisure time, more efficiency, less work, and more "freedom" to be creative.

But I must take issue with this idea that something more convenient is therefore more desirable. There is no room in the movement toward a simple life for the uncreative person or one unwilling to take risks.

I wonder what kind of "powerful sign of simplicity in life style" our Indian visitor saw lacking in our home as he smiled and said, "Ah, yes, you Americans must have everything very convenient."

For the past two years John and Norman have been looking at farms for use by our church, but interest by the congregation in such an idea has diminished. In the process of looking our two families have caught the "farm bug," and last week we found land that we could afford in the mountains of West Virginia.

No one has occupied the farm for 15 years, so there is no end of work to be done, but it is a lovely spot. The old farm house, close to 150 years old, has pegged windows and hand-hewn foundation beams. Many of the weathered out-buildings are crumbled piles of boards and shingles. The land is rocky and full of broom sage, but we are all convinced it has possibilities.

This is the first time we have owned a house or land, and it is an awesome responsibility. It creates some practical problems for us, but overriding this is a feeling of anticipation and excitement.

Life these days seems anything but simple. When someone asked Kathy what her daddy did she replied, "Oh, he just goes to meetings." Books are stacking up waiting to be read, my loom waits to be warped, and I'm beginning to resent the traffic pattern that constantly flows through our house. John's deepening interest in the whole area of nonviolence and peace lies dormant because of lack of time for study. We both want time to work on family relationships. Our children are growing to be teen-agers and we find family life drawing the short straw. Both of us are working, and communication more and more occurs via messages taped to the refrigerator door. "Karen, put the casserole in a 350° oven at 5:30. Tell Mike to take the dog to the vet. Find out when Mark will be home tonight."

That long phone cord I had installed has gotten to be a grotesque symbol of hectic living. We can answer the phone and continue to eat dinner. Or I can wash dishes with the phone resting on my shoulder. I still cringe as I recall a friend saying, "Mary, you're banging pots and pans around again. Would you mind giving me your full attention? I really need to talk with you."

So tonight we called the kids together for a family conference. When they were younger they used to think these occasions were great fun and very adult. Now they groan; they're convinced that bad news is about to be dumped on them and resent the fact that John and I tend to do most of the talking. (We'll have to work on that.)

We spent several hours discussing the past eight years of city living and our lifestyle in general. Family consensus is that we will move to the farm. This decision didn't come as a result of anguish or deep personal struggle with the issues of "simple living." Rather it's a practical step we can take to implement some of the decisions we have reached as a family. We are excited about the possibility of taking several years of "early retirement" while our children are still with us and able to experience and enjoy rural living.

Simple life is a mind set. It is a life lived in such a way that one has control over body, mind and spirit. It is a life lived in such a way as to discern how all living things hang together in a delicately woven chain—the plan of a loving Creator. It is a life that necessitates few material possessions. It enables one to experience the freedom to be oneself. It loves people and uses things. Simple life stresses cooperation instead of competition and strives to exploit no person or group of people.

Phil Berrigan in *A Punishment for Peace* writes, "Man after all, needs very little to be man: he needs necessities for sustenance, community for friendship, room for contribution, hope of acceptance on both sides of the grave."

A letter from Tim and Starr confirms the fact that Tim has accepted the call to teach in a seminary in Hong Kong. They are leaving their suburban parish and will spend the next two years studying and learning Mandarin. Their two young sons will have the experience of starting school in Hong Kong. "We are all healthy and happy," Starr writes. "The boys are saddened by the fact that their dog must stay behind but as they say 'We're handling it well, aren't we?' They're very cavalier about announcing 'We're moving to China' to sales clerks who pat their heads and say 'Oh, I don't think so, honey.' Their needs are simple—food, a bed, and us. We have sold our house and most of our possessions. I can't describe the sense of freedom we are feeling, being free of possessions."

And that brings me to Philoxenos, a Syrian who had fun in the sixth century, without benefit of appliances, still less of nuclear deterrents. . . .

"I will not make you such rich men as have need of many things," said Philoxenos (putting the words on the lips of Christ), "but I will make you true rich men who have need of nothing. Since it is not he who has many possessions that is rich, but he who has no needs."

Obviously, we shall always have some *needs. But only he who has the simplest and most natural needs can be considered to be without needs, since the only needs he has are real ones, and the real ones are not hard to fulfill if one is a free man!*

THOMAS MERTON

Thoreau said it beautifully: *"We are as rich as our ability to do without things."*

The children need school shoes so we made one of our infrequent trips across the mountain to Staunton. Usually being tempted by the glitter of new gadgets and latest style in fashion, we were delighted to come home from our trip unscathed, congratulating ourselves that we could say, "Isn't it nice we don't *need* any of this!"

There is a sense of freedom in this attitude. Of course, I'm always ready to shoulder my guilt load again and can be easily persuaded that my new-found truth is demonic. I listen to the convincing argument that if I don't consume things, unemployment will result and the economists will begin to worry. This argument is an insult to our corporate imagination and creative powers. Surely we can design systems that are more satisfying, creative, and humane. Such jobs could contribute to saving the environment, adding beauty to our lives, and enriching us spiritually.

E. F. Schumacher points this out in his book, *Small Is Beautiful* and adds that economists are saying such a thing can be accomplished. It is simply that we choose not to, that we lack the will to try.

I should learn that when you're a guest for dinner, it isn't the best policy to get into a heated discussion about economics, but I really get angry when I'm called un-American because of my strong feelings against "conspicious consumption." I do not believe that "more is better." How far can Detroit push the sale of cars when 200 million people own 129 million vehicles? These cars use irreplaceable fossil fuels, pollute the air, and consume enormous resources when they break down and require repairs. Surely the extension of such growth is logically absurd—not to say intolerable.

Just as we have learned that the uncontrolled growth of cells in the body unchecked by natural restraints, produces the intense pain, decay, and waste we call cancer, so it is time to learn that the "more is better" philosophy is dangerous to our health. Any change in our economic system will cause pain and social dislocation, but each of us has to draw the line somewhere and say "I, for one, will not add to the problem or take responsibility for the death throes of an obsolete economic system."

Marketplace minds are not limited by race, creed, color, or sex, but primarily they belong to women since women are the chief consumers in our country. I sometimes feel helpless when I am bombarded with the powerful force of advertising.

Talking with friends last night we concluded that marketplace minds result from boredom (just as overeating does), from lack of anything meaningful to do with one's life, from the desire to be in style, the need for one-upmanship, or from a fear of not conforming to accepted standards befitting one's background or position in life.

Is it really naive to take Jesus at his word? "I will supply all your needs." (He didn't say: "all your *greed*.")

Maybe my consumer instincts are really a faith problem.

Economic interdependence seems to make such good sense in the day of rising costs. There should be some sensible small step that a group of people could take, short of communal living or shared pay checks, which probably don't appeal to vast numbers.

We watch with interest the attempts of a group of our friends in Washington, D.C. who are trying a limited measure of economic interdependence. It began when Dunstan said, "Unless someone is a waffle freak, why do we all have to own a waffle iron?"

From this first suggestion, the idea of sharing has grown. There is one aluminum extension ladder shared by half a dozen families. Child care is shared. (Margaret says she groans when Wednesdays come because it's her day to entertain the 10 kids). Several families use one washer and dryer. It has progressed to the point where several families share one car—a practical idea, especially in a city where public transportation is available and gas prices and parking problems create headaches. This is, of course, where problems become acute, as there are various approaches to the level of care and cleanliness afforded an automobile. Records, books, plants, and talents are all shared.

Obviously there are problems to interdependence. Some are merely logistic, some deal with how each family views the discipline of children, and some are in the realm of trust and economic fairness. But it seems worth the risks for a group of people to at least try this form of simplifying their lives.

A lot can be said for bartering. This is a way of sharing gifts, of easing the economics of living, and it can be fun. Any service, talent, or commodity can be exchanged for another service, need, or commodity.

Today Bob and Anne brought us 300 pounds of flour they had milled from their wheat. Some of this flour I shared with Eve and Tom in exchange for several gallons of honey from the bees they keep. By helping a neighbor butcher a hog, we received several months supply of lard. Flour, honey, lard—three necessary ingredients that create the miracle of bread I bake to share with Bob and Anne.

Christian simplicity is not scrupulosity about possessions. It is a joyous freedom regarding them.

VERNARD ELLER

Fellowship magazine arrived today. It is an issue devoted to simple life. An article by Robert Aitken was very helpful as we continue to wrestle with the whole concept of ridding ourselves of excess material baggage. Aitken writes:

The hermit may score high as a simple person, but his lesson is hardly instructive for the householder who is seeking a job in order to feed a bunch of hungry children. The kids are making a racket, so do we eliminate them? The "perfectionist" would do just that, I suppose, one way or another.

The simple life is a path of order. It is an arrangement of things. It is a mastery within circumstances. If my purpose as a host is to serve tea, I will need a control of time and place. I will need things at hand: stove, tea kettle, cups or bowls, the tea itself, plus a knowledge of how to prepare and serve, and friends ready to receive and drink.

There may be occasions when it would be appropriate to say, "Oh it is simpler not to have tea." But it is not always appropriate to say this, for we would then be denying ourselves communion, the fabric of life.

If circumstances and things control us, we are overcome by what we call complexity and encumbrance. It is important for us to choose, as best we can, and in co-operation with others, appropriate order.

Lanza Del Vasto, disciple of Gandhi, and leader of Society of the Ark, puts it succinctly: "How can we work against oppression? Today there is much talk about the big business interests, the polluters, the war machines. But when *you* buy something do you ask, 'How was it made?' or 'How does it have such a small price?' or 'Does it represent the work of an oppressed people—the oppressed of an entire class or a country?' Don't blame the exploiters—blame yourself. Without you, they cannot go on. Then they'll say, 'Well, make it yourself!' And you'll discover that you *can* make it yourself—or do without."

December 26: Christmas was fun. Again this year we had looked forward to the Advent season and of course Christmas. But at no other time of the year is the whole materialism game more obvious. We weren't certain that the idea of simple life could overcome the strong images built up over the years in the minds of the children regarding the number of toys, clothes, and "things" which constituted Christmas morning around the tree.

Our first indication that perhaps the kids had really understood what it was all about was Mike's Christmas list, traditionally taped to the refrigerator door. "New tennis shoes, a pair of warmer pajamas, and some embroidered designs on my jeans or blue shirt." (Sometimes the kids amaze me.) That seemed to be the green light to proceed with our alternative Christmas plans.

I will in no way delude myself into thinking that the kids had suddenly become non-materialistic. Mark still wants a car of his own; they all want new records; and though clothes are not high on their priority list, anything new is always appreciated. They are normal, middle-class teen-agers, but it seems to me they were very happy over the way Christmas was celebrated this year.

Again we followed the old Austrian custom of drawing Advent friends. Each of us secretly did for one other member of the family something very special. Dishes got done without asking; ground pine from high up on the mountain appeared on the mantle and around the windows; and chamber pots mysteriously got emptied. The brass Advent wreath with store-bought candles of past years was replaced with orange juice container candles which Kathy made. She displayed them on random height pieces of birch, surrounding them with laurel and pine. Hemlock boughs got tacked to the privy walls, making it the sweetest smelling outhouse for miles around.

We set about writing a Sunday school Christmas program that I had been asked to direct. We baked breads, and cookies, and rosettes for friends: for a neighbor who keeps our 1960 Scout truck going when John gives up all hope and accepts its demise; for Anne who sees that we get our mail; for Galen who plowed our one-mile lane when snowstorms isolated us; for farmers who had shared their cabbages, knowledge, time, and sausage with us.

Relatives received floating walnut-shell candles, and candles with pressed leaves and dried weeds, shelled walnuts and butternuts, and dried apples in old blue canning jars. Karen and Kathy made dozens of tree decorations using dried natural materials. The bark of sweet birch was scraped to make wintergreen tea.

Del Vasto's statement "Make it yourself—or do without" seems harsh and extreme, and the first time I read it I was angry. I am not such an idealist or anti-manufacture snob that I want to give or receive only hand-made gifts, but I am becoming more aware that there are ways to stop the contagion of consumerism.

Alternative Christmases and birthdays take extra time and some creative thinking. Without my knowledge Karen somehow found the hours to make me an unbleached muslin blouse—her first attempt at such a project. Kathy struggled to learn a new Christmas carol on the piano to share with us on Christmas day. The boys spent hours secretly sanding and polishing a beautiful wild cherry coffee table they had made, admitting that it was more exciting to give the gift to us than to receive their own.

Creativity and improvisations are fringe benefits of reduced income.

Kings may have made their way bringing gifts that first Christmas, but for us it was more like a shepherd's gift.

A snowstorm the week before Christmas had almost incapacitated us. Being fairly new to potbellied stoves, we were not aware of how quickly they gobble up wood. The supply in the woodshed was dwindling, but we assumed we could always chop some as the need arose. This was not true. We looked at the meager supply left on the porch, at the drifts of snow and our malfunctioning Scout truck, and realized how foolish we had been.

We had scarcely finished Christmas breakfast when we saw Theodore's truck slowly making its way through the drifts of snow. It was loaded with wood for our stove.

"Just got to thinking that you might need this," he explained as he began unloading his truck. "I didn't want to interfere, but last time I was over it didn't look to me like you had enough wood to last you through the week."

I half expected him to yell, "Merry Christmas to all and to all a good night," as his truck disappeared down the lane.

Our 1960 truck had surely been around the world twice before we bought it. John spends much of his free time under the truck, replacing, repairing, greasing, tightening, and mumbling. Not being able to afford a new one, we coax, plead, and nurse the Scout along. Even a red and yellow daisy pasted on the back which reads, "Celebrate Life" did nothing to pep up its spirit.

John remarked yesterday that for him the simple life would include a new four-wheel drive vehicle. It just confirmed the fact that "simple life" isn't all that easy to define.

In some ways the high-rise apartment dweller with a basement parking space, shops on the lower level, maintenance man available, swimming pool and elevator, leads a very simple life—if we mean by a simple life, the lack of worry about our daily necessities.

If simple life does not have a dimension of global justice, ecological integrity, and a communal dimension, then those of us who could afford it would merely find the most convenient way to live.

There are those individuals and groups who are developing lifestyles consistent with the path of peace and Christian concern. The Shakertown Pledge group is attempting to live under the following covenant:

Recognizing that the earth and the fullness thereof is a gift from God, and that we are called to cherish, nurture, and provide loving stewardship for the earth's resources,

And recognizing that life itself is a gift, and a call to responsibility, job and celebration, I make the following declarations:

1. I declare myself to be a world citizen. (or I recog-

nize that I am a world citizen and that all the people of the earth are my neighbors.)

2. *I commit myself to lead an ecologically sound life.*

3. *I commit myself to occupational responsibility. I will seek to avoid the creation of products which work others harm.*

4. *I commit myself to personal renewal through meditation, prayer and reflection.*

5. *I affirm the gift that is my body, and pledge that I will attend to its proper nourishment and physical fitness.*

6. *I pledge myself to examine continually my relations with others and to attempt to relate honestly, morally, and lovingly with those around me.*

7. *I commit myself to responsible participation in a community of faith.*

8. *I commit myself to leading a life of creative simplicity, and to share my personal wealth with the world's poor.*

9. *I pledge myself to join with others in the reshaping of institutions in order to bring about a more just global society in which each person has full access to the needed resources for their physical, emotional, intellectual and spiritual growth.*

A letter from Dora is always a welcome addition to my day. This one admonishes me to practice what I preach. "You're still busy, busy, busy," she wrote. "How come you've neglected your weaving?"

I admit to myself that I am still hung up on the need to impress our many guests with a clean house, well prepared meals, and a garden free of weeds. I want to make sure there is fresh bread and plenty of wild strawberry jelly.

These things are not what impress me when I am in the role of guest. I wonder why I think it's required of me as a hostess? How much better to give one's self to guests by deep interest in them, taking time to listen and share, and being refreshed enough to be genuinely happy they are with you.

I remember Lee telling us at the pastors' wives retreat last month that we are to save our best hours and energy for our husbands. Lee was serious and didn't even smile when we all groaned. Cathy pointed out that she has three small children in diapers. I'm sure Lee is right. Cathy is in a bind because three children usurp her energy, but I don't have that excuse anymore.

Perhaps someday when I understand what simple life is, I will learn to slow down, to enjoy, to be creative, to give myself freely to others.

Everyone needs a Dora to remind her that middle-class values and "it's expected of me" excuses are not really valid.

There is more to life than increasing its speed.

GANDHI

I think back to a conversation with Pat. She says that for her, simple life implies a necessity to slow down, a "letting go."

I made a banner once that said, "Slow me down, Lord," but I gave it away because I was uncomfortable with it hanging in the hallway where it kept getting knocked down as we hurried past.

I keep wondering if Martin Luther actually did spend twice as much time in meditation and prayer when he had an especially busy day.

Milton tells us that when he was a missionary in India, the Indian name for an American meant "in a hurry man."

It is not a new or profound insight, but Pat's comment serves as a reminder to me that to enjoy the moment, the person at hand, the place, the time, to enjoy who I am—this is part of the fullness of life Christ came to bring us.

I struggle daily with my impatience and my insensitivity to others who seem slow to understand, who can't find things quickly or who interrupt my plans for the day. I think I need to list "slowing down" under the simple life.

It seemed like a romantic idea—making maple syrup. Surely such an activity can qualify as belonging to the simple life. This activity takes cooperation, lots of buckets, a good stand of maple trees, old wood to keep the fires hot, and plenty of time.

Thirty to forty gallons of sugar water will make about one gallon of syrup, so the old copper kettle we had borrowed was filled to the brim several times a day. Sometimes we would still be skimming the syrup and watching it boil until eleven at night. I suppose Mike and Kathy and I looked rather ridiculous late one night sitting in front of the fire, watching the syrup and catching snow flakes in our mouths. Those silly, happy times are the fringe benefits of the simple life.

Continuing to boil maple syrup creates other maple products. Cooked to a soft ball stage, it produces a chewy maple candy, then come the "clinkers"—that brown, brittle confectionary, followed by the sudden appearance of maple sugar. The bubbling and boiling becomes intense, and a grayish brown crystallized substance appears at the bottom of the kettle. I am told that in days past the sugar was left in one solid lump and broken off as needed.

I told friends from the city that I had put the sugar in the blender to make it granulated. They broke out laughing, and Carolyn said I had shattered the entire romanticism of simple life.

Just another inconsistency in our life. We use a blender but have no indoor toilets.

Yesterday was a day at the beach. It was a working day, however. I had been asked to serve as a consultant for a church council retreat. The group wanted to discuss the "hippie culture" in their neighborhood and how their church could best relate to these young people.

One of the council members had opened his beach home for the retreat, and the group was enjoying the setting. They wore old, comfortable clothes or bathing suits and enjoyed the feel of the warm sand on their bare feet.

My first observation as a consultant was to point out that they could not really minister to the youth culture around the church until they had come to terms with their anger. There were protests and a general denial that they felt any anger. I replied that I thought anger was inevitable. They were a group of men who worked hard— many at jobs they didn't enjoy—in order to have a few days a year enjoying their old comfortable clothes and going barefooted. How could they help but be angry at a group of kids who somehow managed to live that way all year long!

One of our nearest neighbors who lives in the next

"holler" offered to spray our potatoes for us. We hastened to explain that we were organic gardeners and preferred not to use chemical sprays and fertilizers on our vegetables.

"It can't be done," our neighbor warned. "The bugs will win the battle."

I pointed to the rows of marigolds, zinnias, and garlic interspersed between the beans and broccoli. "The odor of these is supposed to keep the pest population down," I explained.

"And I suppose you come out at midnight and do a little dance by the light of the full moon," he retorted, spreading out his arms and giving his hips a wiggle.

I observe countless mercies, kindnesses and much cooperation in nature, and I maintain that it is these that typify nature rather than the violence and competitions. My studies have gradually led me to the conclusion that it is the cooperative rather than the competitive that survives. The meek do inherit the earth.

EUELL GIBBONS

"I believe that God has created me and all that exists. . . . Therefore I surely ought to thank, and praise, serve and obey him."

Being an earth caretaker hardly ranked very high on our priority lists until about 10 years ago. I had never heard the word ecology or pollutant used in sentences, much less given thought to how we were treating the environment that sustains us and gives us life. I simply assumed this good gift called earth would continue to give, and give and give to supply my needs. I gave no thought to the fact that it takes hundreds of thousands of years for a can or bottle carelessly tossed in the ditch to become dust once again. I assumed that the god called technology would come to the rescue when fossil fuels, tin, copper, fresh water, or a variety of sea life disappeared from the earth. Debates over the use of nuclear power plants, aerosol spray cans, and the amount of time we have before our fresh water supplies are gone need never have occurred had not the desire for bigger, better, faster, more convenient ways of living been our goal.

To take peace as a lifestyle, we must ask ourselves if we can continue the present use of natural resources, waste water and energy as we have been doing just to maintain our comfortable, convenient patterns of living. Before I point a finger elsewhere I need to look much more closely at my own consumption patterns.

I believe that a desirable future depends on our deliberately choosing a life of action over a life of consumption, on our engendering a lifestyle which will enable us to be spontaneous, independent, yet related to each other rather than maintaining a lifestyle which only allows us to make and unmake, produce and consume—a style of life which is merely a way station on the road to the depletion and pollution of the environment.

IVAN ILLICH

The Contemplative Vision

It has become more and more clear that any sustained quest for peace will include a contemplative vision. I would never have used the term "contemplative" to describe myself and hesitate even hinting at it now. The writings of Thomas Merton have been of the most help in this regard and have freed me up a little so that I'm not quite so uncomfortable with the term.

Merton says in *New Seeds of Contemplation:* "The worst disadvantage of this word is that it sounds like 'something,' an objective quality, a spiritual commodity that one can procure, something that it is good to have, something which when possessed, liberates one from problems and from unhappiness. As if there were a new project to be undertaken, among all the million other projects suggested to us in our lifetime—to become contemplatives."

It is difficult for us to learn that the contemplative vision is an awareness, not a method. We confirm our misunderstanding when we continue to look for something else to read about contemplation instead of emptying ourselves and leaving ourselves open for the Spirit to work.

One of the dangers in using the term contemplation is that it implies for most of us a kind of ecstasy and a measure of mystical union. But the heart of contemplation is to value what seems common and routine. The contemplative finds God in what is, in the ordinary, not above and beyond the things of this world. In other words, our basic difficulty is that contemplation is too simple for us to understand, not too complicated.

I've been invited to lead a retreat for pastors on the subject of contemplation. As is too often the case, I had delayed my preparation too long and now felt pressured. Just several days prior to leading the retreat I set aside my morning for planning and writing. It took until ten in the morning for me to realize the inconsistency of the subject matter and my own circumstance and attitude. I was writing on contemplation and hadn't even noted the beauty of the late winter day. In the midst of books and words, in the confinement of a room, I was writing about awareness, receptivity, and beauty.

I closed the books, put on a warm coat and went outside. For about an hour I gathered sugar water from the buckets hanging on our maple trees. I started a fire and began to boil down the water. Only then did I *see* the beauty of the mountains, sheep on a far hill, cloud formations against the sky. Only then did I *feel* cool air on my face and life in my body. Only then did I *hear* trees groaning in the wind and birds calling. Only then was I aware of our loving sheep dog who enjoys life and was so thoroughly pleased that someone she loves had come outside the house and into her world.

I don't consider myself a romantic or anti-intellectual. I was aware, however, that it took this move away from the notes and books before I was aware of God's presence and in something of a contemplative mood. I spent the rest of the day outside. I think it was better preparation for leading the retreat.

RAIN: *Let me say this before rain becomes a utility that they can plan and distribute for money. By "they" I mean the people who cannot understand that rain is a festival, who do not appreciate its gratuity, who think that what has no price has no value, that what cannot be sold is not real, so that the only way to make something actual is to place it on the market. The time will come when they sell you even your rain. At the moment it is still free, and I am in it. I celebrate its gratuity and its meaninglessness.*

THOMAS MERTON

The children were fascinated by the knowledge Theodore has acquired in his 65 years, and we soon learned to love him and lean on his expertise as we tackle the multitude of new farm experiences. He finds joy in everything around him. He can sit for hours watching a squirrel build a nest or gather acorns. He imitates the call of birds and catches bees in his calloused, bare hands, knows where the best streams are for "gigging," and in five minutes time can pick us an armful of weeds from pokeberry to lamb's-quarter, that can be used as greens for supper. He knows every kind of flower, tree, and animal track. I have watched him pick up a rough dirty board from behind the maple sugar house and fashion beautiful, wormy chestnut trim boards for our kitchen windows.

But Theodore's greatest joy in life is communicating with his friends. That is why it seems such a tragedy that a year ago surgery for cancer removed his larynx, leaving him speechless. In a way his voicelessness has served to heighten his powers of observation and his enjoyment of life around him that many of us fail to note or heed.

He would deny the label "contemplative" even more than we would, but he lives a contemplation that needs no label to authenticate it.

By definition a contemplative is one devoted to prayer. At first glance I thought this solved my difficulty with the word contemplation. It was merely the fancy word to describe prayer, and if I took away the fancy label, I'd eliminate my difficulty. But we have the same troubles with the word prayer as we have with contemplation. Actually, it can be a freeing thing to begin to talk about contemplation. We have tended to encrust prayer with complicated methods and structure. Even when we have as simple an understanding as "talking with God" we are not without our problems.

Thomas Merton had such a difficult time convincing people that prayer did not involve more complicated methodology. Just before he left on his trip to the Far East in 1968, a small group of people met with him and asked him to speak to them on prayer. Merton responded:

Nothing that anyone says will be that important. The great thing is prayer. Prayer itself. If you want a life of prayer, the way to get it is by praying. . . . The whole thing boils down to giving ourselves in prayer a chance to realize that we have what we seek. We don't have to rush after it. It is there all the time, and if we give it time it will make itself known to us. . . . The real contemplative standard is to have no standard at all, to be just yourself. . . . I believe that what we want to do is to pray. O.K., now pray. This is the whole doctrine of prayer in the Rule of St. Benedict. It's all summed up in one phrase: "If a man wants to pray, let him go and pray." That is all St. Benedict feels it is necessary to say about the subject. He doesn't say, let us go in and start with a little introductory prayer etc. If you want to pray, pray. . . . If we really want prayer, we'll have to give it time . . . we must learn to "waste time" conscientiously.

My times of prayer must be first of all moments of honesty. Certainly prayer is more than being honest with myself, but I'm afraid we haven't started there and that's disastrous. Prayer is an opening to reality not a flight from it. Contemplation is observing the world in which we live and our life as it is. We see the world and ourselves through the eye of the gospel—but it is the real world and our true self. Too often our prayers are attempts at escape and our saying and feeling the things we know we ought to say and feel. When we feel dishonest inside, we can be sure it isn't really prayer. In prayer all things are stripped of duplicity and compromise.

Contemplation is to be dis-illusioned.
Illusion comes from the Latin word *ludere* meaning "to play." Illusion, or living with an illusion, is games playing. To play games is more comfortable than to deal with

the reality of the way things are. If I am dis-illusioned, I become honest with myself and stop playing games. We have accepted so many illusions about life, the world, values, ourselves. To be dis-illusioned is to begin to see things as they really are. A contemplative life style is one in which the dis-illusioning process carries over more and more into my daily thoughts, feelings, and decisions.

Jim Carrol continues to say what I wish I had said, or at least in ways that I wish I could say it. I think he's my favorite poet. I can still picture him reading from his black notebook late into the night. Maybe it's because we shared the experience of the '60s together that he seems to make so much sense now.

His new little book, *Contemplation,* has many helpful ideas. He shares with Merton many similar ideas about the contemplative vision. For Jim, contemplation is not seeing some different thing but rather a different way of seeing. He also speaks of the need to be dis-illusioned:

Mortification calls into question the perennial human assumptions around which men are always dancing—that suffering and pain are to be avoided at all costs; that consumption of things, pleasures, and experiences makes a person happy and the more one consumes the better off one is; to sit still is to waste time; the goal of life is to have; whatever (or whoever) is old is obsolete, while whatever (or whoever) is new is good, indeed better; permanent commitment is impossible and undesirable; drugs (from alcohol, to acid and aspirin) are good things; sexual liberation means love is the only rule; being radical means denying what went before.

Contemplation involves an attitude of receptivity. For

most of us this receptivity will serve to diminish or at least balance our desire to manipulate. The contemplative has the capacity to accept what comes rather than a need to always manage the outcome. This attitude enhances and enriches life especially at those points where we cannot change the circumstances and waste a lot of time rebelling against reality.

I'd like to be a contemplative on our next automobile trip. Then when the car breaks down in some small town, I'll enjoy having some time to explore that part of the country and to meet some new people.

Last time I was anything but contemplative. I fussed and fumed the entire time our car was being repaired and wasted a day. Next time will be different—but it will have to be by the grace of God. This kind of contemplation comes hard for me.

In a visit this morning with one of our neighbors, I casually asked how things were going. His answer is noteworthy as an indication of his philosophy of life.

"Well, I had my teeth set for lots of corn this season but the Lord saw fit to give us cucumbers instead. So I'm enjoying the cucumbers."

Maybe that's what Gandhi meant when he said that no matter where one lives, one should live with a rural mind.

My brother seems upset by the fact that I wash clothes with a wringer machine, scrub board, and tub. He has offered to put in the pipes for an automatic machine.

I look forward to the hours I spend doing this twice-a-week chore. It has become my private meditation period. You might call it "redeeming the time." The added bonus of farm wash day is the wonderful fragrance that clothes hung on a line, exposed to sun and wind (and sometimes snow and rain) bring into the house with them.

One aspect of contemplation is silence. We know that it is more than the absence of sounds, but we often fail to experience what it really is. I don't experience silence, even when I'm all alone on the mountain in almost total absence of sounds, if my mind is racing with thoughts and concerns. On the other hand, I have experienced moments of silence in the midst of the sounds of a busy city street.

The mystics tell us there are three stages of silence: silence of the tongue, silence of the mind, and silence of the will. This helps some, but even more helpful is a description of anti-silence: anything which numbs the senses and the Source of life.

We treated ourselves to a restaurant meal last night. The Greek cafe was crowded as usual. The food there is good and inexpensive, but the atmosphere is a little hectic. Tables are pushed close together to accommodate the crowds and we could hear conversation in different languages around us.

Perhaps that is why it was so obvious that at a table close by there was no conversation at all. A middle-aged couple ate their entire meal in complete silence except for one question about the *baklava*. It was sad to note they had nothing whatsoever to say to one another, no smiles that said "I love you," or looks that shared the secrets of many years.

When silence means there is nothing to communicate, it is the outward evidence of an inner emptiness. But there can be a deep sense of communication that needs no sound or words.

How comfortable it is to be in the presence of someone with whom you feel a deep sense of oneness, with no need to communicate verbally. I tend to be one who feels the need to fill in the "silence gaps" with chatter, as if there will be some embarrassment if a minute goes by without something being said—like the proper hostess, making sure the guests are circulating and socializing.

Being with Pat is always refreshing. We share a lot of conversation but there is a relief at being able to just be quiet—weaving, embroidering, or sharing a cup of coffee in silence.

Silence can be a lack of communication or a very deep level of it.

The Spirit too comes to help us in our weakness. For when we cannot choose words in order to pray properly, the Spirit himself expresses our plea in a way that could never be put into words, and God who knows everything in our hearts knows perfectly well what he means, and that the pleas of the saints expressed by the Spirit are according to the mind of God.

ROMANS 8:26 JB

SIGHS TOO DEEP FOR WORDS
Like ourselves when we try
to love each other
air blows cold and hot.
We are left wondering
if our passions were mistaken,
if our loneliness is, in the end,
everything. And God?

Like ourselves when we are
distant and close at once,
He confuses us. Like ourselves,
He begins his story with an
eye-catching title, then
fools us, fading, leaving us asking
if this pain we cannot avoid
though we try
is yearning after Him or
yearning only after yearning.
Is God my pious name for guilt?
As the doctor keeps telling me
by the way he holds his head.
You ask, "How do you pray
when it's all so foggy?"
But it's not foggy at all,
don't you see?
It is as clear as air; prayer.
How I pray is breathe.
I remember the poet Paul
who couldn't shake the faith either
saying, "Praying? Forget Praying!
The spirit, breath of God, lives
in you, in your bones, in your heart,
interrupting God for you all day.
Relax. Don't worry about it.
The spirit prays for you with
sighs too deep for words."
Paul, baby, I could kiss you
for those lines which
come I suspect more from your
insane desire like mine
than from any facts you had.

90

Sighs like that I know about.
If you tell me those sighs
are the breath of God praying
I can believe it. I can believe it.
My sighs are warm and cool,
death and life, far and near.
My sighs always surprise me,
for a sigh is what happens when
the breath I breathe is not all mine.
How I pray is breathe,
knowing the air that brings the world
into my soul escapes its hedge
with more of me
than I knew was there.

JAMES CARROLL

91

Peace Is a Lifestyle

Shalom is a new "in" word. It is a popular subject for conferences, retreats, articles, and books. One should be pleased that the study of peace is becoming popular, but I have reservations. Somehow the popularization process always takes away sharp edges. When the cross became popular costume jewelry, it could hardly portray the "scandal" anymore. Someone will find a way to make shalom a commercial success and in the process empty it of its hard realities of justice and righteousness. My greatest fear is shalom will be sold as a local anesthetic, numbing us in happy tranquility, causing us to forget the nagging issues of poverty, hunger, oppression, and racism.

A realistic look at the situation in the world today brings any thoughtful person to a keen awareness of the necessity to face up to some urgent problems. When we confront these problems, we should be aware there are some things we think *about* and other things we think *with*. The things we think *with* are more basic. They are the "givens" for us, our basic assumptions. We don't often challenge these things because they have become settled over a period of time and have been firmly established through teaching and experience. The present global crisis challenges us to look again at those basic assumptions. The biblical concept of shalom may well form the basis for the things we think *with*.

Shalom is a rich word. It is always difficult to define words that carry a depth of meaning. Shalom is a way to say hello and also a way to say goodbye. It is a greeting and a benediction. It refers to the total well-being which a person desires for oneself and for others. It also refers to unity, justice, righteousness, security, and prosperity.

A word that means so many things runs the danger of losing its meaning. This is true of the English word "love." But it is possible to study the biblical use of shalom and then to conclude it has some major themes. One of these themes is the interdependency of all things. Our universe is one delicate web, everything is connected to everything else.

Walter Brueggeman writes in *Signs of Shalom,* "The central vision of world history in the Bible is that all of creation is one, every creature in community with every other, living in harmony and security toward the joy and well-being of every other creature."

Paul writing to the Colossians includes the cosmos itself in the redeeming work of Jesus. "Through him God chose to reconcile the whole universe to himself, making peace through the shedding of his blood upon the cross

94

—to reconcile all things, whether on earth or in heaven, through him alone" (Col. 1:20 JB).

But even more prevalent in a biblical study of shalom is the theme of justice. Larry Rasmussen of Wesley Theological Seminary in Washingotn, D.C. presented a paper on shalom at the Order of St. Martin meeting. Especially significant for me were his words about justice: "Well-being is biblically unthinkable apart from social justice and is tied especially to the inclusion of the excluded. Community well-being is given its litmus test against their condition."

When the Spirit is poured on us, righteousness will prevail. "In the wilderness justice will come to live and integrity in the fertile land; integrity will bring peace, justice give lasting security" (Isaiah 32:16-17 JB).

Where do I start in a vocation of peacebuilding? This is a continuing question for many people. I'm sure there are many valid answers, but one starting point emerges more and more clearly as the one necessary for me. It's at the one place where I have the most chance of exercising change—my own lifestyle. I won't work for the changes necessary for justice and peace if these changes are inconsistent with my own values. In other words, the basic change must come in the things I think *with*.

I will not take on the task of unmasking the world's illusions unless I seek to be disillusioned myself through a contemplative vision established in a discipline of daily prayer.

I will not work for the necessary steps of ending the arms race if my basic personal security is in the adequate defense of my home with firearms and security measures to deter any possible invader.

Global justice will come to me as a threat to be resisted if I have not separated my needs from my greeds and determined that I am not really free until I can share the world's good with hungry brothers and sisters.

I will not advocate the very necessary changes in the care of the earth and respect for its limited resources until I have become detached from my dependence upon convenience and consumption as the basis for my happiness and contentment.

We must be wary of ourselves when the worst that is in man becomes objectified in society, approved, acclaimed and deified, when hatred becomes patriotism and murder a holy duty, when spying and delation are called love of truth and the stool pigeon is a public benefactor, when the gnawing and prurient resentments of frustrated bureaucrats become the conscience of the people and the gangster is enthroned in power, then we must fear the voice of our own heart, even when it denounces them. For are we not all tainted with the same poison?

That is why we must not be deceived by the giants, and by their thunderous denunciations of one another, their preparations for mutual destruction. The fact that they are powerful does not mean that they are sane, and the fact that they speak with intense conviction does not mean that they speak the truth.

THOMAS MERTON

The Quakers have done some further statistical analysis on the armament situation. Today's mail brought the summary of a study which shows:

The nations of the world have spent $4.5 trillion ($4,500,000,000,000) for "military security" since 1946.

This year they will spend upwards of $240 billion for "military security."

The United States accounts for over 1/3 of all military expenditures on the planet.

The nuclear arsenal of the United States now holds the equivalent of 615,000 Hiroshima-sized bombs, enough to annihilate every major Soviet city 36 times. The Soviet Union can level every major American city 11 times.

How much will it take until we feel safe?

"Until the Lord watches over the city, the watchman stays awake in vain" (Psalm 127:1).

No Hunting signs greet visitors at our first gate. The signs did little to endear us to neighbors who for years had used our acreage as public hunting grounds. Deer venture close to the house most evenings, and wild turkeys strut across the hillsides somehow knowing they are safe here. Our neighbors have respected our desires, however. Though they may disagree and think it strange, they have abided by our decision.

Today a truck drove up in the rain and the driver demanded of Mark that his parents come out and talk with him. Since John was gone, I went out to greet our visitor. He refused my invitation to come into the house, so the conversation proceeded with me standing in the rain, peering through a half-open truck window.

"I just want you to know," the heavily bearded man began, "that I have hunted on this property all my life and I intend to keep doing so!"

I introduced myself and asked his name. "I don't have a name. They just call me number three," he mumbled.

"Oh, come on," I smiled, "everyone has a name. You're

certainly important enough to be called something other than number three."

Then I realized this must be the man neighbors had warned us about. I kept wishing John were around and felt foolish that my heart was beating so quickly.

He continued to reinforce his message. "I intend to come up here with my gun and dogs, and there ain't nothing you can do to stop me!"

"You're right," I said. "There is nothing I can do, but I would hope you would respect our wishes."

He didn't seem to hear and was shouting now. "You can shoot me or call the sheriff if you want, but I'm still going to hunt on this property!"

"No, we would never do that. We don't even own a gun. We only ask that you respect our 'no hunting' signs." I was very wet and shivering, but he seemed to be running out of steam. He began stretching and yawning, never looking me in the eye.

"Well, I can send my dogs across your land to drive the deer off and then shoot them on the other side of the line fence," he said casually.

"Yes, you could, but I don't think you will," I responded.

The man stared ahead for a few minutes, started his truck and mumbled as he rolled up his window, "Well, I certainly hope you'll be happy here. It's a good farm."

He drove off down the lane. We have seen him several times since. He comes to the farm occasionally to "look things over," but he never has his gun.

The biblical vision of Shalom functions always as a firm rejection of values and lifestyles which seek security and well-being in manipulative ways at the expense of

*another part of creation, another part of the community,
or another brother.*

WALTER BRUEGGEMANN

The church proclaims to American society that it is
possible to do good and also to do well—to live a life
of moral integrity and also prosper materially, continuing
to live in comfort.

Shalom has such a rich dose of justice that this proclamation must be shown as a false gospel. It is something
like the false prophets in the Old Testament who cried
"peace, peace" when there was no peace.

In order to live lives of faithful integrity we should
listen to the proclamation "Do good, even if we don't
do well."

Sign at the entrance of a church operated conference
center:

MEET GOD'S CHALLENGES IN COMFORTABLE
SURROUNDINGS

*Find out how much God has given you, and from it
take what you need; the remainder is needed by others.
The superfluities of the rich are the necessities of the poor.
Those who retain what is superfluous possess the goods
of others.*

ST. AUGUSTINE

The ethicists are talking *triage* again. This time it is in
connection with who will be fed, but it's still the old
dilemma. I think it has to be examined.

In the war years, triage (sorting out) referred to the
policy by which medical assistance was given. It was up

to the doctors to "color-tag" the wounded, placing them in one of three categories according to their condition. One color meant hopeless—nothing we can do will save them. Another tag meant they'll make it whether they get help or not. The third color-tag indicated a doubtful prognosis—a chance to live only if medical assistance is given. Since there were limited medical supplies and resources, assistance was given only to this last group. It sounds reasonable, but I think we'll have to remember Lou.

Lou was badly blown apart, including one leg severely wounded. The doctor who examined him made the decision that Lou was a hopeless case and tagged him as such, leaving him to die. But a nurse noticed Lou was conscious and began to talk with him. They discovered they both were from Ohio. Getting to know Lou as a person, the nurse just couldn't let him die. She broke all the rules and changed his color tag.

There followed a two-day trip in the back of a truck and months in a hospital. But Lou made it. He met a girl in the hospital who later became his wife. Even minus one leg he has led a full happy life, all because a nurse broke the rules of triage and changed a tag.

Maybe the task of the church is going around changing the tags. Maybe that's what Jesus meant to tell us when he touched the leper. Perhaps our clearest lifestyle call is to be with the outcasts and the ones society has labeled hopeless.

Conditional living is one of our most dangerous traps. Conditional living says when certain outward circumstances change, then I'll function the way I was created to function. When the kids are grown, when I have a less demanding job, when my salary is adequate, when this particular project or assignment is completed, *then* watch and see how I live fully, maturely, unselfishly, lovingly. It's a lie! It would make peace a point of arrival, rather than a way of traveling.

This evening at dinner we played a kind of "do you remember" game. It began when Mark commented on how lucky we were to have all the clean air which surrounds our mountain farm and the clear, unpolluted streams where we can fish and swim. We all agreed it was a blessing for which we could be truly thankful, but then we started thinking about the people trapped in large cities. As we began comparing rural and city life, we began to think of simple pleasures unique to city living and the "do you remember" game began.

Do you remember the fountains we splashed in; the alley where we rode our bikes (and how the apartment manager kept coming out to scold!); the ice cream truck with its soft bells; the time the sun set at the end of Newport Place, looking like a gigantic orange ball in the street; hop-scotch and four-square games on the sidewalks; the rubbing we made off a manhole cover; the corner store for soda and gum; how everyone sat on the front steps on hot summer nights and visited with one another; bike rides along the canal; the smell of the coffee shop in Georgetown; zoos and museums and galleries within walking distance of our home?

The list went on and on, but mostly it centered on remembering people. We could only conclude that simple, abundant life does not depend upon place or circumstances. It depends upon a mind set—how one views life.

An incident was related to me today and I'm still reflecting upon it. A Protestant minister visited a Roman Catholic monastery. In the course of his visit he was introduced to one of the monks and knew him to be a liturgical scholar. The minister asked what he had been doing the past year.

He fully expected to hear the focus of the monk's latest research. But the answer startled him. "Mostly helping Brother Sebastian die."

The answer was strange enough to cause the minister to think he had not heard correctly so he responded, "What did you say?"

The monk then gave a little further explanation. "Oh, I have done some study and writing. But Brother Sebastian was 83 years old and was dying. So I spent most of the year helping him die."

I wish we could have the priorities in our own life and in the ministry of the church where this incident would not be quite so rare. If we could eliminate some of our intense pressure to be "productive," perhaps we could be more faithful. Instead of giving only a final verbal blessing of shalom to a friend, perhaps we could spend a year or so helping him die, or at least a few hours helping him live.

A friend heard we were writing a book on peace. He said he hoped it would be a "how-to" book. "The world has too many books on the concept of peace but too few on how you do something constructive to work for peace," he said.

I indicated my personal conviction about starting with our own lifestyle, about changing our value systems and the way in which we live as a first step.

He was disappointed in this approach. He had in mind certain programs or projects. We didn't come to any agreement. He may be correct about our starting point being naive, but he also agreed that perhaps he wanted a way to change the world without the necessity of any radical change for himself.

The '60s seem long ago, but they are still vivid in our minds as we now view these journal entries. The peace we sought then was largely the cessation of the armed conflict in Vietnam—a *pax romana*. We would do the same thing again, in fact we hope even now we are working to avoid a resumption of fighting.

But there has been considerable growth in our understanding of peace. Shalom is broader than the absence of war. As we look back to the peace movement, it was a quest for peace. What is really needed is a peace quest. This seems like such a subtle difference, but it is critical.

Peace is a lifestyle. Peace is not a goal at the end of the journey, it is the way we walk. As is so often true, we therefore have moved into a clearer understanding of what we already knew, or should have known.

Jesus still says to us, "Would that even today you knew the things that make for peace!"

For Further Reading

Many books could be listed dealing with the topics we have included as "Things That Make for Peace." We have chosen a few in each category which were especially helpful to us.

Peace and War

Bainton, Roland. *Christian Attitudes Toward War and Peace.* New York: Abingdon, 1960.
A basic historical background to the various attitudes within the Christian tradition regarding the peace/war question.

Brown, Robert McAfee. *Religion and Violence.* Philadelphia: Westminster, 1973.
Noteworthy because of the number of key issues with which it deals. The reader will find new insights into

the nature of violence, the various attitudes within Christendom concerning the peace/war issue, the possibility of criteria for a just revolution, aspects of global injustice, and the essence of nonviolence exemplified by Gandhi, Martin Luther King, and César Chavez.

Potter, Ralph B. *War and Moral Discourse*. Richmond, Va.: John Knox, 1969.
A scholarly work by an ethics professor. It is a recapitulation of the arguments concerning justified and unjustified use of violence. The book provides the moral discourse for a just war position largely on the basis of justice and our neighbor's welfare.
There is a very helpful bibliographical essay as an appendix. A detailed history of the pertinent articles and books over the past 30 or 40 years provides a comprehensive bibliography for one who wants to study further.

Yoder, John Howard. *Nevertheless*. Scottdale, Pa.: Herald Press, 1971.
A Mennonite scholar and teacher analyzes 25 varieties of pacifism to show that there is no one pacifist stance.

_____. *The Original Revolution*. Scottdale, Pa.: Herald Press, 1971.
Especially helpful for an understanding of the Mennonite position on church-state relationships.

_____. *The Politics of Jesus*. Grand Rapids: Eerdmans, 1972.
The most comprehensive of Yoder's books, it examines the assumption that Jesus is a political, social, and economic radical from the basis of the New Testament.

106

Nonviolence

"The Sermon on the Mount" (Matthew 5-7)

Our understanding of nonviolence is based on the life, death, and teachings of Jesus. The authors listed below also cite this as the basis or cite the more theological phrase, "the theology of the cross."

Douglass, James W. *The Non-Violent Cross*. New York: Macmillan, 1969.

A powerful proposal of revolutionary action through nonviolence. Written by a Roman Catholic layman, the book is deeply rooted in the Judeo-Christian tradition.

Ellul, Jacque. *Violence*. New York: Seabury, 1969.

Ellul is an eminent social critic and lay theologian whose books are challenging and provocative. After he has provided a convincing proof of the necessity of violence, he proposes as the essence of Christian freedom, the ability to deny the necessary.

Merton, Thomas, ed. *Gandhi on Non-Violence*. New York: New Directions, 1965.

This small volume will whet the appetite for some study of Gandhi; it is an excellent starter and sample of his philosophy.

King, Martin Luther, *Strength to Love,* New York: Harper and Row, 1963.

Martin Luther King, Jr. provided America with a clear example of a nonviolent lifestyle. This book of sermons provides one way to learn more about this man and the faith he lived.

Yoder, John Howard. *Original Revolution and Politics of Jesus* (already mentioned under "Peace and War").

Global Justice

Brown, Lester. *By Bread Alone*. New York: Praeger, 1974.
One of the most comprehensive studies of the world food crisis.

Goulet, Denis. *The Cruel Choice*. New York: Atheneum, 1973.
An analysis of the various concepts of development. After reading Goulet's book, it is somewhat easier to understand why the recipients of our "development" are rejecting it in favor of a theology of liberation.

Schumacher, E. F. *Small Is Beautiful*. New York: Harper and Row, 1973.
The author lives up to the subtitle discussing "economics as if people mattered." This excellent book deserves wide acceptance.

Taylor, John V. *Enough Is Enough*. London: SCM Press, 1975.
This book is confrontive, easy to understand, and painfully difficult to misunderstand. The subject of excesses —food, goods, wages, prices, pollution, armaments and the like—is the theme of the 115-page paperback. Anglican Bishop Taylor speaks to these issues with a "theology of enough." This thoroughly biblical theology may be one of the keys for discovering the new freedom that awaits us in a world of increasing scarcities.

Simple Life

Brown, Edward. *The Tassajara Bread Book.* Berkeley Cal.: Shambala Publications, 1970.

For beginning or experienced cooks who want to make excellent, nutritional breads and pastries. I include it because bread making is one way to begin to enjoy the simple life. There is something very satisfying about participating in the miracle of yeast and bread.

Emery, Carla. *Old Fashioned Recipe Book.* Published by the author in Kendrick, Idaho, 1975.

600 pages of "back to the earth" information from milking goats to making soap, food preservation, recipes, animal care, home remedies, tea from herbs. Fun to read even if you never intend to make your own baking powder or blankets from deer skins.

Jacobson, Michael. *Nutrition Scoreboard.* Washington, D.C.: Center for Science in the Public Interest, 1973.

Our whole family has enjoyed browsing through this informative paperback. Categories of food are rated according to their nutritional value. Mike was upset that Morton coconut cream pies were listed with the "junkyard foods," but Kathy was delighted that Cap'n Crunch rated above oatmeal.

Kelly, Thomas R. *Testament of Devotion.* New York: Harper and Row, 1941.

A look at the chapter titles gives a hint to why we consider this book of devotional reading so helpful: The Light Within, Holy Obedience, The Blessed Community, The Eternal Now and Social Concern, The Simplification of Life.

Lappe, Frances Moore, *Diet for a Small Planet*. New York: Ballantine Book, 1971.

As stated in the foreword, "This book is about protein—how we as a nation are caught in a pattern that squanders it; and how you can choose the opposite—a way of eating that makes the most of the earth's capacity to supply this vital nutrient." This somewhat controversial book leads the reader to see how one can improve your lifestyle and at the same time help our very small planet. A good help for those who are willing to change their eating habits.

Leopold, Aldo. *A Sand County Almanac*. New York: Ballantine Book, 1966.

An environmental classic. A sensitively written book dealing with a lifestyle that protects and appreciates our created environment.

Mesarovic, Mihajlo and Pestel, Eduard. *Mankind at the Turning Point*. New York: Dutton, 1974.

This second report of the Club of Rome makes its major contribution by confronting us with the immensity of the global crises—population, natural resources, food, water, and environmental pollution. Experts debate the accuracy of some of the computer scenarios, but no one disputes the reality of these crises facing mankind.

Contemplation

Carrol, James. *Contemplation*. New York: Paulist Press, 1972.

James Carrol continues to be one of the refreshing and provocative spokesmen for our day. Through his articles, stories, and poems he speaks to and for those who are attempting to make some sense out of chaotic times.

Merton, Thomas. *New Seeds of Contemplation*. New York: New Directions, 1972.
Merton provided the primary inspiration for the chapter on contemplation. This volume will no doubt some day be listed as a classic in the field of contemplative literature.

Nouwen, Henri, *Pray to Live*. Notre Dame, Ind.: Fides, 1972.
An excellent introduction into the thought of Thomas Merton. Nouwen believes that for Merton the way to relevance was the way of prayer and contemplation. By carefully selected passages, the reader is introduced to this theme.

Nouwen, Henri. *Out of Solitude*. Notre Dame, Ind.: Ave Maria Press, 1974.
Three brief and profound meditations on the Christian life. It becomes clear why Nouwen could so readily understand Thomas Merton: it is because both men are contemplatives.

ACKNOWLEDGMENTS

Our thanks to the following for permission to quote from published materials:

American Friends Service Committee, Inc. for quotations from the statement, *Speak Truth to Power.*

Fellowship magazine for quotations from Robert Aitken.

Herald Press for quotations from John H. Yoder, *The Original Revolution* (Scottdale, Pa.: Herald Press, 1971), p. 29.

Macmillan Publishing Co. for quotations from James W. Douglass, *The Non-Violent Cross* (copyright © 1967, 1968 by James W. Douglass).

Monastic Studies for quotations from "Recollections" by Thomas Merton.

New American Library for quotations from Maria de Jesus, *Child of the Dark.*

New Directions Publishing Corp. for quotations from Thomas Merton, *Emblems of a Season of Fury* (Copyright © 1963 by The Abbey of Gethsemani, Inc.) and *Raids on the Unspeakable* (copyright © 1966 by The Abbey of Gethsemani, Inc.).

Paulist Press for James Carroll, *Elements of Hope* (copyright © 1971 by The Missionary Society of St. Paul the Apostle) and *Contemplation* (copyright © 1972 by The Missionary Society of St. Paul the Apostle).

Henry Regnery Co. for quotations from Martin Luther King in *The Pacifist Conscience,* ed. by Peter Mayer.

The Shakertown Pledge Group for The Shakertown Pledge.